YOUR
CHAKRA
PERSONALITY

About the Author

Shai Tubali, PhD, is an international speaker, author, and spiritual teacher, recognized as one of Europe's leading authorities on chakras and the subtle body. He has authored twelve books, now translated into thirteen languages. Alongside his writing, Tubali is a researcher in the philosophy of religion at the University of Leeds and has developed several meditation-based therapeutic methods. Visit him at ShaiTubali.com.

To Write to the Author

If you wish to contact the author or would like more information about this book, please write to the author in care of Llewellyn Worldwide Ltd. and we will forward your request. Both the author and publisher appreciate hearing from you and learning of your enjoyment of this book and how it has helped you. Llewellyn Worldwide Ltd. cannot guarantee that every letter written to the author can be answered, but all will be forwarded. Please write to:

Shai Tubali
℅ Llewellyn Worldwide
2143 Wooddale Drive
Woodbury, MN 55125-2989

Please enclose a self-addressed stamped envelope for reply,
or $1.00 to cover costs. If outside the U.S.A., enclose
an international postal reply coupon.

Many of Llewellyn's authors have websites with additional
information and resources. For more information,
please visit our website at http://www.llewellyn.com.

SHAI TUBALI

YOUR

CHAKRA

PERSONALITY

Discover Your Soul Design
through PRIMARY &
SECONDARY CHAKRAS

LLEWELLYN
WOODBURY, MINNESOTA

FIRST EDITION
First Printing, 2024

Book design by Samantha Peterson
Cover design by Shannon McKuhen
Interior illustration by Llewellyn Art Department

Llewellyn Publications is a registered trademark of Llewellyn Worldwide Ltd.

Library of Congress Cataloging-in-Publication Data (Pending)
ISBN: 978-0-7387-7771-9

Llewellyn Publications
A Division of Llewellyn Worldwide Ltd.
2143 Wooddale Drive
Woodbury, MN 55125-2989
www.llewellyn.com

Printed in the United States of America

Other Books by Shai Tubali

7 Day Chakras

A Guide to Bliss

Indestructible You

The Journey to Inner Power

Llewellyn's Complete Book of Meditation

The Seven Chakra Personality Types

The Seven Wisdoms of Life

The Transformative Philosophical Dialogue

Unlocking the 7 Powers of the Heart

To Alaya, a magnificent blend of
daughter and lifelong friend.
May you embrace the full blossoming of
your chakra personality, flourishing like the
beautiful flower you are in the cosmic garden.

CONTENTS

PRACTICES

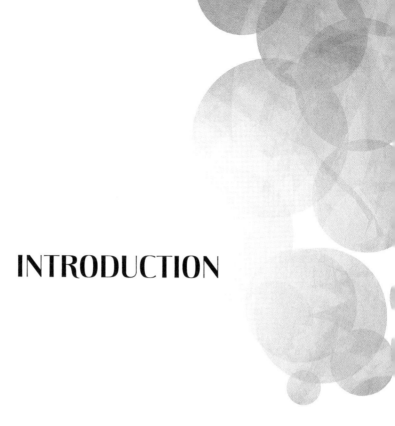

INTRODUCTION

This book takes you on an exciting journey to understand who you really are using the wisdom of the chakras. It's not just a book to read—it's a tool to help you discover yourself and grow as an individual. You'll view the chakras in a new way as you explore their role as active forces that shape your worldview, personality, and spiritual growth. You'll also learn how each chakra plays a part in who you are and how they work together to create the whole you.

This book serves as a practical guide to help you understand your "soul design," which is the unique energy pattern that makes you *you*. By figuring out this pattern, you'll learn a lot about your strengths, your weak spots, and what motivates you in life. This knowledge will help you find a balance between accepting who you are and aiming to grow. It guides you toward a life that truly matches your deepest self.

How This Book Came to Be

On the journey of self-discovery and spiritual growth, some moments can change our lives and reveal hidden parts of ourselves. In 2002, I experienced one of these moments when I met Dr. Gabriel Cousens, an American yogi from the sacred Nityananda tradition. I spent the next seven years learning from him. He shared ancient wisdom about Kundalini, the chakras, and the subtle body, which went beyond what is usually seen or understood. I didn't realize then that this meeting would enhance my understanding of human nature and lead me to create a new way to describe personalities, called "the chakra types."

The Nityananda tradition, which is rooted in the rich soils of India, revealed a world previously unknown to me: one where the activation of the subtle body held the key to higher spiritual purposes. Prior to this, the world of chakras had remained shrouded in mystery, their significance eluding my grasp. But through this initiation into the luminous world of the subtle body, the chakras ceased to be mere concepts, instead revealing themselves as living energy centers within me. Their pulsating presence became tangible, their wisdom accessible, and the reality of their transformative power unfolded before my very eyes.

Initially, I only scratched the surface of the implications and applications of the chakra system. Traditionally, chakras are mainly regarded as seven energy centers that function as a ladder of spiritual transformation, along which the practitioner awakens dormant states of consciousness. But chakras, I came to realize, were also associated with *samskaras*—deep-rooted imprints that we carry with us from the past—and *vasanas*, our personality tendencies. Moreover, each chakra housed specific abilities, skills, wisdom, and life lessons.

As I collected this information and listened intently to the chakras alive within me, I had a revelation: *the chakras are a comprehensive map of a person's psychological landscape.* If I wanted a complete picture of my psychological development and maturation, all I had to do was take a look at my chakras and their themes and resolutions. This led me to a subtler realization: chakras serve as gateways to the full spectrum of human experience. Representing seven aspects of our being, they became the keys to unlocking the seven dimensions of life itself.

Over time, I discovered that the chakra system encompassed a personal and individual dimension. It became evident that chakras were not merely a uniform ladder of development, prescribing how everyone should ascend through the universal layers of their being. In reality, everyone possesses some chakras that are stronger than others as well as some that are weaker. While chakras can be "stronger" or "weaker," this is by no means a form of imbalance that needs to be corrected. Inherently strong chakras are actually powerful energy centers; energetically speaking, they are filled with greater intensity, and for a good reason. These chakras are the hidden forces that shape the way a person perceives the world and the way their personality eventually forms.

I came to realize that each of us is guided by the specific perspective, qualities, and values of one primary chakra. Drawing on my understanding of chakras and harnessing the power of imagination, I attempted to visualize what a personality emerging from a certain chakra would look like. How would this chakra behave, act, and live if it were a human being with a complete and vibrant identity? As I immersed myself in this creative process, I found myself crafting elaborate descriptions that felt vivid and real. To my delight and astonishment, it became effortless to identify these descriptions within myself and those around me.

However, people are complex, and I found that one chakra alone could not encompass an individual's entire personality. By closely observing individuals, studying their worldviews, and analyzing their reactions, it became clear that there were three main chakras whose interplay gave rise to the multifaceted nature of one's personality. These three main chakras were a person's chakra type. This realization was enlightening, as it uncovered the energetic patterns that underlie the formation of one's personality.

An Inborn Energetic Pattern

As you read, you might have intuited that chakra types do more than merely lay bare one's personality. Indeed, chakra types hold a power that extends well beyond the realm of personality revelation alone. You see, the term "personality" itself is a deceptive label, for individuality is shaped not only by internal traits but also by external influences, such as societal pressures and cultural and familial conditioning. It is within this intricate tapestry of existence that one's personality forms. While the chakra types system serves as a typology that classifies personalities, its true essence delves much deeper.

The chakra types system reveals the energetic blueprint that accompanies one's journey in this world.

As you navigate the path of chakra development, you will occasionally feel the pull to focus on specific chakras. You might sense the need to nurture your heart chakra, cultivate strength in your solar plexus chakra, or ground yourself by tending to your root chakra, for example. This periodic attention to specific chakras aligns with your holistic growth. Whether or not you are aware of the principles of chakra development, you will instinctively recognize the internal call to address certain areas of your life. However, unlike transient concerns, your chakra type is an unwavering companion throughout your life, an inborn energetic pattern that shapes your hidden constitution and gives rise to your unique personality.

In many ways, your chakra type is akin to the body you inhabit throughout your existence. While you can make superficial alterations and even undergo drastic transformations, you cannot discard your body and trade it for a new one. Likewise, each of us has a chakra type that remains a constant presence, steadfast amid the ever-changing stages of development. It is through this enduring pattern that we gain fundamental insights into the depths of our being.

You may worry that being classified by a chakra type limits you to a specific identity. It's natural to want to believe in unlimited potential. Yet, if you look closely at your life with total honesty, you will see clear and consistent patterns. Now, why should adhering to a pattern be regarded as a negative trait? When we observe the consistent patterns exhibited by flowers, mountains, and butterflies, we do not wish for them to be anything other than what they are. We appreciate the beauty inherent in their form. In fact, it is precisely these patterns that lend meaning and magnificence to these phenomena. Each possesses its rightful place in the world. Embracing this sentiment, one of the central principles of understanding chakra types is learning to accept, love, and harmonize with your own pattern.

Allow me to share a delightful anecdote. During a chakra types seminar that I presented in the Netherlands, I invited participants to engage in a group sharing session as we neared the end of the program. One gentleman, who had remained relatively silent until that point, took a seat before everyone and candidly confessed his struggles with resistance throughout the weekend.

He declared, "I vehemently rejected being put in a box. I longed for independence and freedom from the perceived limitations of this structure." With a touch of irony, he added, "Then I came to the realization that I am, in fact, a sacral chakra type." The room erupted in laughter, for one of the defining traits of a sacral chakra type is their aversion to confinement. As fiercely independent beings, they rebel against the constraints of the world. This insightful individual recognized that even resisting conformity to a pattern was, in itself, an expression of a pattern!

The key to a balanced approach lies in understanding that, regardless of the pattern you follow, your profound sense of identity should remain untethered and limitless. The pattern itself serves as a tool, a conduit through which you channel your innate tendencies. Your chakra type is not a new identity; rather, your inherently free being necessitates certain patterns to express and manifest itself. By embracing this equilibrium, one sheds the fear of being boxed in and discovers a liberating path instead.

Consider your chakra type pattern as a form of service to the world. Your chakra type serves as your compass, enabling you to find your rightful place in the grand tapestry of existence. It becomes the key to feeling at home within yourself while selflessly contributing to the world around you. With this realization, the so-called box transforms from a stifling enclosure into something that sets us free.

Unlocking the Gifts of the Chakra Types

Within the expansive realm of the chakra types system lie five profound gifts awaiting your discovery. The first gift, hinted at previously, is the gift of self-understanding. By delving into the blueprint of the three energetic forces that shape your personality, you will unlock a profound understanding of yourself. You will gain insight into why you behave and react in certain ways. This self-understanding transcends the personal, aligning you with the grand plan of nature, the universe, and life itself.

The second gift bestowed upon you is the gift of balance. Armed with the awareness of your inherent constitution, you will gain the power to harmonize its excesses. By understanding your inborn tendencies, you can prevent them from overflowing and spiraling into self-destructive patterns. Through this self-understanding, you will become adept at harnessing these forces, taming behavioral patterns, and even alleviating the grip of obsessions and compulsions.

The third gift is the precious treasure of fulfillment. To embrace fulfillment is to uncover the path toward your true potential. Everyone possesses unique avenues of self-realization and manifestation. To fully embark on these paths, you must first discern what you are meant to fulfill and how you can bring it to fruition. This profound awareness guides you toward a life of purpose and wholeness.

The final two gifts bestowed upon you by the chakra types system reside within the realm of emotion, entwined with love and compassion. The fourth gift is the ability to truly love yourself. Yet this love surpasses superficial sentiments or a general sense of self-acceptance—it is a love grounded in understanding: an understanding of your pattern, the exquisite flower that you are. It encompasses the recognition of your strengths and limitations, acknowledging what you can be, what you cannot be, and what you already are. It also entails discarding the burdensome expectations of what you "should" or "should not" be. You will learn to relax into your authentic self, emancipating yourself from the influence of external voices, including any critical inner chatter.

The last gift awaits you in the boundless expanse of *compassion*, which radiates from the heart to encompass all those around you. Once you grasp the profound truth that others, too, are following their unique pattern, this realization leads to genuine compassion. No longer will you scrutinize anyone through judgmental eyes, yearning to mold them. Instead, you will understand that they are meant to be exactly who they are, as they are following their own path of self-realization. When you understand the chakra types, you will relinquish the need to impose your chakra type upon others, instead embracing the beauty and diversity of individuality.

As you embark on this transformative journey, the chakra types system grants you these extraordinary gifts. Through self-understanding, you will find balance, fulfillment, and a profound love for yourself. And by embracing compassion, you will extend your understanding to all, celebrating the uniqueness of each individual's journey. This harmonious integration of self and others unlocks the true essence of the chakra types, transforming life into a radiant masterpiece of authenticity, purpose, and love.

Determining Your Soul Design

In the not-too-distant past of 2018, I introduced the concept of chakra types to the world in my debut book, *The Seven Chakra Personality Types*. This innovative framework resonated with readers, guiding them away from confusion and toward authenticity. This current book, however, is far more nuanced than the introduction to the seven primary types offered in my initial work. *Your Chakra Personality* is an exploration of your distinct three-type constitution.

Uncovering your primary chakra is a pivotal first step, a revelation in itself, yet it is merely a single thread in the rich fabric of your chakra makeup. As such, I begin this journey by establishing an understanding of each primary chakra type, paving the way for subsequent chapters to delve into the intricate weave of your primary, secondary, and supportive chakra types.

The depth of understanding that can be found in the seemingly modest chakra-types blueprint is astounding. All it takes is a contemplative moment to set in motion a profound journey of self-discovery. When you scrutinize the interplay of your primary, secondary, and supportive chakra types, it's as though a veil lifts, revealing the architecture of your personality and the unseen forces that sculpt it, animate it, and guide it toward its destiny. This process illuminates more than just your personality; it also nudges you to confront your internal contradictions and conflicts, those shadowy tenants that dwell within your psyche.

By embracing this framework, you're not simply gifted a map, but a compass—a guiding light that can shepherd you through life's terrain. Your chakra type invites you to return, time and again, to the immutable blueprint of your being, to ponder its implications, to explore its depths. This blueprint is not just a constant reminder of who you are. It's more like a coded scroll, revealing its profound wisdom gradually, measuredly, as time's patient hand unrolls it. Over the years, your structure will continue to reveal itself, like a masterful epic.

As you explore the multifaceted nature of your chakra type system, the significance of your primary type should never be obscured. This central chakra remains the cornerstone of your most authentic self. Visualize your primary chakra type as the sun around which your secondary and supportive chakra types revolve, like celestial bodies in the cosmos. In light of this importance, we will begin with an introduction of the seven primary chakra types. I'll share their unique characteristics and illuminate how each functions as a secondary and supportive type as well. To me, elucidating the seven primary types is akin to composing a heartfelt poem for each vibrant hue of the human spectrum. When I playfully touch upon a type's idiosyncrasies or seeming limitations, remember that this is no different than appreciating the imperfections in a single flower or any other marvel of nature. Each type, each color, each bloom, holds an essential place in the grand design.

At the beginning of chapter 2, you will encounter a questionnaire. This tool will, in most cases, reliably assist you in discerning your primary (and occasionally secondary) chakra type. However, the subtler nuances of your supportive chakra may remain elusive, and the lines between secondary and supportive chakras can blur. While you journey through this book, revisit this questionnaire periodically, refining your responses as your self-awareness expands.

Identifying your primary and secondary chakra types often proves simpler than accepting them. Acceptance can be elusive, sometimes hindered by resistance rooted in factors discussed in chapter 3. If you face such challenges, embrace them as part of the rewarding process of self-discovery. Indeed, this is the profound journey all of us are destined to traverse. Revel in the process, taking the time to savor each step. Allow yourself the luxury of patience as you discern your primary, secondary, and supportive types. This is not a race, but a gentle waltz with self-awareness, as each step brings you closer to understanding your energetic blueprint.

Bear in mind that your primary chakra type might not align with your aspirations or self-perception. You may yearn to be recognized as a heart or sacral chakra type, only to realize that these desires stem from deep-seated inhibitions. Recognizing and understanding these inhibitions is a key step toward genuine self-understanding.

What Your Blueprint Can Do for You

Your primary chakra type influences your desires, shapes your passions, and scripts the experiences that profoundly resonate for you. It outlines what you are destined to represent in the world and defines the authentic expression of your soul. Simultaneously, your primary chakra type serves as a template for your core struggles and your emotional and mental patterns.

Identifying your primary chakra type is, accordingly, a twofold process. The first step is an inward journey to your heart's desire, acknowledging what stirs your passion and what you genuinely love to be and do. It's essentially about pinpointing what feels like home. Any attempt to fit into a different chakra type would feel forced and inauthentic, like wearing a garment tailored for someone else. Your primary chakra type should feel natural, aligning perfectly with your fundamental worldview.

The second step in identifying your primary type involves confronting the unique, personal tug-of-war that you engage in with the world. I call this your "life theme," an integral concept that will be examined and experimented with in chapter 4. Your life-theme is akin to a narrative thread weaving through the tapestry of your existence, highlighting the friction between a pair of contrasting forces. What's truly intriguing is that this tension is born from the heart's deepest yearnings. It springs forth from the well of passion within you, aligning with your chakra type, but its fulfillment invariably involves a dynamic interaction with the world—an interaction that's often filled with challenges and struggles, hence its description as a tug-of-war. From this tussle between your passion and the world, your life-theme emerges, encompassing your personal journey, the struggles and triumphs, the lessons and growth. It becomes the poignant story of your life.

Learning your primary chakra type will highlight your main tensions and key psychological issues. It works both ways: by understanding the main tension within yourself, you can figure out which chakra type is the strongest in you. This interesting topic will be discussed in greater detail in part I of the book.

While the primary chakra type plays a vital role in one's life, the true brilliance of the chakra types method is revealed in its triadic structure and the relations within it. As you read this book, you'll construct a blueprint that aims to answer three pivotal questions:

1. Who are you, not in terms of identity, but in relation to your deepest passions, intentions, and motivations?
2. What is your purpose in this life?

3. How are you meant to actualize your unique gifts and abilities? What propels you forward on your journey?

Discovering your chakra blueprint provides an understanding of the fundamental tensions that ripple through your personality and life. It uncovers the energetic origins of the internal discord that pulls you in multiple directions. For example, you'll learn that a significant cause of conflict in life is the rivalry between the primary and secondary chakra types. As they both vie for dominance, you'll frequently need to remind yourself that only one can reign in your personality.

The chakra blueprint's second benefit is its ability to guide you toward the right choices. Understanding the different desires within you illuminates your path and the steps you should begin to take. Essentially, you will grasp the various forces within you as well as their designated roles.

The blueprint's third offering is its potential to foster acceptance of your structure, including its so-called "defects." You'll learn that these perceived flaws do not need to be improved, changed, or eliminated. Rather, they need to be harnessed correctly to prevent a self-destructive spiral.

Every primary chakra type carries certain excesses, limitations, and strong tendencies or even obsessions. The beauty of the three-type structure lies in its ability to balance and refine these aspects, sometimes even facilitating their expression. Without this balancing mechanism, we would merely be exaggerated embodiments of a single type. Thankfully, this complex structure softens the sharp edges and provides empowerment when necessary. Conversely, the complexity of the three-type structure also introduces some tensions and imbalances that demand your attention, which keeps things interesting.

The Journey within This Book

This book will guide you on an exhilarating journey with three distinct steps. Each of these steps will include suggested writing and visualization exercises to deepen comprehension and inspire introspection. The exploration of the chakra types unfolds gradually, urging you to savor this knowledge. You might not grasp all the subtleties within the first few chapters; hence, patience is crucial (unless your disposition is inherently impatient, making this journey a bit more of a test).

As outlined previously, part I of this book focuses on acquainting you with the seven chakra types, guiding you to locate your primary chakra type. This journey of self-discovery will be facilitated via four distinctive practices. Even in the face of potential confusion or uncertainty, you will venture into discussions about self-identification, hurdles you might encounter, doubts you may harbor, and the eventual assimilation of the primary chakra into the three-chakra-type structure.

In part II, you will delve deeper into the three-type structure. The goal is to understand the importance of each of the central chakras (the primary, secondary, and supportive chakra types) and their respective roles within this structure. Then, you'll journey through the forty-two possible pairings of the primary and secondary chakra types. Each of the forty-two types work together to illuminate sources of happiness and meaning, thereby directing you toward fulfillment and self-realization. This book does not examine all 210 three-chakra combinations, as the complexity might prove overwhelming; however, I have provided examples of the three-type structure.

Also in part II, you'll set your sights on crafting your blueprint, taking the first tentative steps toward deciphering the mysteries of your chakra type. You will seek to unlock your blueprint's wealth of information and harness its full potential. To hone and refine this skill, I have provided sample blueprints. If you wish to become a proficient practitioner of this system, mastering the art of interpreting others' blueprints is a necessity. I also share a plethora of case studies and engage in their analysis. This stage promises a stimulating mixture of challenge and delight.

In the third and final part of this book, you will devote your effort to understanding the tensions and conflicts that exist within, primarily between the primary and secondary chakra types. Armed with accrued knowledge, you will learn to manage and resolve these internal disputes. You will discover what it truly means to ease into your primary chakra type, how to handle your life-theme from within your primary type, and how to identify the strengths and weaknesses inherent in your chakra-type structure. You will learn how to leverage these strengths, balance the imbalances, and channel your energies toward fulfillment. Essentially, you will learn to enable all three aspects of your chakra type to function harmoniously as a community rather than as isolated entities. At the end of part III, I address what life might look like when navigated according to this blueprint, and what it means to live life with an awareness of this structure.

So, dear reader, I extend a warm invitation to join me on this luminous journey of exploring the chakra types—revelations that blossomed from seven years of dedicated research. Within these pages, you will find a blueprint to understanding the depths of your own being and uncovering the profound influence of the chakras on your personality, your relationships, and the very fabric of your existence. Embark on a voyage that promises to shift your perception of yourself and the world around you, forever.

ONE

THE CHAKRAS

You may have begun this book with full or partial knowledge of the chakras. If that is the case, your reading experience will build on this solid foundation. You may also have been drawn to this book without prior knowledge of the chakra system. Perhaps you have simply been guided by an intuition that this journey can help you better understand yourself and supply you with answers to some of the most critical questions in your life's journey. If the latter description fits your reader profile, this chapter will be an important aid in introducing you to the chakras. However, even if you are well versed in the chakra system, you are likely to derive some fresh insights from this brief introduction.

Start by Feeling Your Chakras

Even if you do not have any intellectual knowledge of the chakras, you know what chakras are at other, more instinctive levels of your being. Sometimes chakras appear to be an esoteric concept, accessible only to fervent believers. But, in reality, chakras are far from a theory. This system is a deeply felt reality inside your body, here and now.

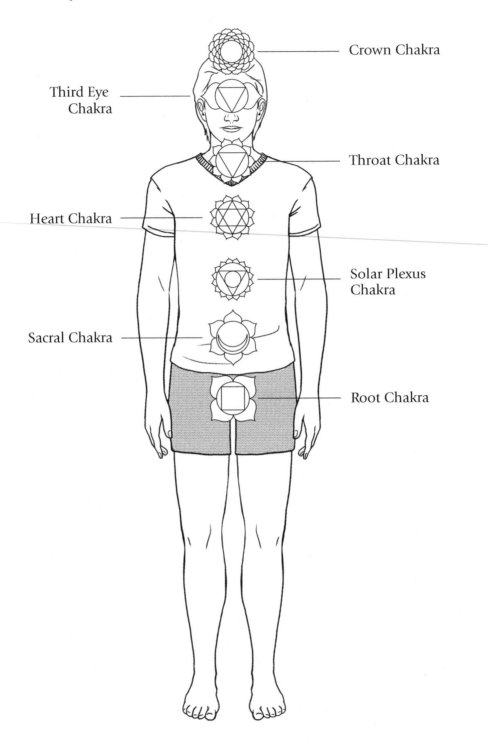

Crown Chakra

Third Eye
Chakra

Throat Chakra

Heart Chakra

Solar Plexus
Chakra

Sacral Chakra

Root Chakra

In fact, many people experience their chakras on a daily basis, as they are triggered by and react to different situations. You may know what it feels like to be heartbroken, or that sensation when the solar plexus is under pressure and you are unable to breathe. You may also know all too well what it's like when your legs feel shaky, or when your throat feels suffocated, or when your head feels mentally overwhelmed. On the other hand, you may be familiar with the sense of having an open heart, what it is like to "see" something clearly even when your senses cannot capture it, or the feelings of energy and power in your belly, butterflies in your stomach, your feet firmly on the ground, or a release in your throat after authentically expressing yourself. All these feelings and states arise from the chakras interacting with certain experiences in the world.

The visceral reality of the chakras is one of the main reasons that this system has become so attractive. As opposed to many other dimensions of your spiritual being that rely on a firm belief in abstract notions or elusive energies, chakras feel almost physical. Of course, you will not be able to detect them inside your body—and thankfully so, since none of us want to have our hearts literally break as a result of a breakup!—but their presence is ceaselessly and undeniably indicated by feelings and sensations.

Here is a simple technique to trace feelings and emotions back to their corresponding chakras. It is a part of a method I developed called "Chakra Reflection," which aims to turn us all into chakra whisperers (individuals capable of listening closely to the messages of the chakras). You don't have to have any prior knowledge to carry out the following technique.

1. Close your eyes. Breathe slowly and deeply. Relax more and more with every breath you take. While you are allowing yourself to relax, think about a present challenge in your life. Consider an issue that has been bothering you lately, during recent weeks or even just the past few days.

2. As much as possible, describe the situation to yourself. What is so challenging about it? What questions does it raise? Who are the people involved, and how is your challenge related to them? You may write your thoughts down.

3. Keeping the general challenge in your mind, allow a recent event or moment that triggered this issue to rise to the surface. See this event

or moment in your mind's eye, and relive it in as much detail as possible. Again, you may write these reflections down.

4. Using the memory of the event or moment, get in touch with the emotions, feelings, and sensations provoked by this challenge. To communicate with deeper layers of your psyche, ask yourself, *What does it feel like?* Gradually, examine which areas of your body respond quickly and strongly to the emotions and feelings you have aroused. Look for the one area in your body that has been triggered the most. Take time to let the feelings and energies settle before finally identifying the area of the body involved.

5. While contacting the most stimulated area, move into its core. What does it feel like? Does it feel hot or cold? Is it energetically swollen or congested? Is it sinking inward? Is it suffocated or suppressed? Does it feel like a closed fist? Does it wish to erupt or burst out? And so on.

6. As you are listening to that affected area, you can even attempt to read its energetic messages. What is the underlying issue that is reflected through this body part? Take a moment to jot possible reflections down.

7. You can also examine secondary body centers that are energetically involved in this issue. Is there a general condition they all share? What body areas are not stimulated at all as a result of this reflection? Finally, take a deep breath and calmly open your eyes.

Whatever areas of the body you identified in this practice, they are always chakra-related. Thus, if you revisit this technique while being aware of the emotional themes, lessons, and developmental potential of each chakra, you will be able to easily pinpoint the subtle connections between your experience and the affected chakra. The affected chakra then becomes a way to better understand and handle the challenging situation.

But why is this so? What makes the chakras so deeply intertwined with bodily parts and sensations, feelings, energies, emotional and mental themes, and life lessons? It is because chakras, despite being primarily energy centers, exist on the borderline between all the inner realms: from the physical and energetic to the emotional, mental, and spiritual. Think of the chakras as the go-between; they are the system through which all these realms converge and exchange information. Chakras translate energies into the language of emotion, and thoughts into the language of energy. This is another reason that chakras play a crucial role in human life, one that far exceeds other subtle components within our being.

Chakras, Traditionally Understood

The concept of chakras has been around for thousands of years. They are mentioned metaphorically in classical Indian scriptures, and later, in a more developed form, in various tantric Hindu and Buddhist systems. Nevertheless, one can identify intuitive and allegorical descriptions of chakras in all traditions, including Western monotheistic religions. It is impossible, however, to understand the nature and role of the chakras without familiarizing yourself with the subtle body as a whole.

The subtle body is like a bridge between the sublime dimensions of the spirit and the physical body. For this reason, it is a mixture of both spirit and body, and several of its features resemble the physical body's anatomy and physiology. These commonalities include subtle forms of the nervous system, spine and spinal fluid, glands, and breathing. Additionally, the subtle body can be debilitated and poorly active, or it can be potent and healthy—just like the physical body. As such, the subtle body requires conscious nourishment.

The subtle body is composed of four main components, the first of which is the equivalent of the nervous system: tens of thousands of hollow tubes branching out from one central channel. These tubes (commonly known as *nadis*, although nadis can also be physical, such as blood vessels and nerves) conduct the various subtle energies (*pranas*) used by the subtle body for sustenance and diverse activities. While there are thousands of such tubes, three of them are traditionally focused on and developed: the central channel (in Hindu traditions, the *sushumna*)—which is both the primary nerve-like column and the energetic twin of the physical spine—and two secondary channels that run parallel to it, intertwining around it at certain points. These points are the chakras.

Deeply ingrained in the central channel, the chakras are the main energy confluences of this entire nerve-like network. You can think of them as gland-like centers. Energetically speaking, each chakra not only governs the nerve-like plexuses in its region but also heavily influences the physical nerves, glands, and organs that surround it.

While this book focuses on seven chakras, the number seven is not the ultimate count of the chakras. In fact, the number differs among the diverse traditions that have adopted this system, and it depends on method and purpose. There is little doubt, however, that the most established and widespread classification, which derives from tantric Hindu traditions, is the one that counts seven chakras, starting at the level of the perineum and culminating at the top of the head. The seven-chakra system is particularly effective not only in terms of energy work; for those interested in chakras as a comprehensive map of psychological and spiritual development, this is an ideal model of human existence, capturing our multilayered being from the most material to the most spiritual.

Each chakra may be highly or minimally functional. These two conditions —between which a range of states exists—have been popularly described in terms of "open" or "closed" chakras. Chakras can indeed be clogged up, and for different reasons, due to their multidimensional nature. A primary factor is their emotional health. While each chakra contains its distinct energetic and spiritual potential, it is also strongly associated with unique mental and emotional content. Among this content, you can find deep-seated imprints (in Sanskrit, *samskaras*) such as traumas, personality traits (*vasanas*), and mental activities (*vrittis*) that often lead to an agitated mind. This implies that a chakra may be "closed" as a result of an unaddressed emotional issue, a deeply buried memory, or an unlearned life lesson. Nevertheless, chakras sensitively respond to a myriad of physical, energetic, and spiritual influences. Thus, the way you lead your life can either impede their activity or enable their blossoming.

The chakras' sensitive response to external influences has led to a common New Age belief that chakras can easily be "opened" by merely exposing them to certain stimuli. Some people place crystals over specific chakras, play certain musical pieces, or burn types of incense that claim to heal and unblock these energy centers. These rituals may temporarily enhance the activity of the chakra, but they could never replace the profound energetic, psychological, and spiritual evolution that a chakra requires to fulfill its dormant capacities. It should be remembered that some tantric Hindu and Buddhist systems have devoted voluminous instructions for chakra development, encompassing forms of progressive meditation and visualization, yoga postures and breathing exercises, and real-life tests and practices.

Still, the practices for chakra development can be generally divided into two major types. Since chakras are, after all, energy centers, deep energy work on your chakras can ultimately activate their higher emotional, mental, and spiritual capacities. Most subtle body–oriented traditions, such as the Hindu Kundalini tantra and the Tibetan Kagyu lineage, have focused the attention of their practitioners on these kinds of practices. They have identified mantras (meditation-inducing words or sounds), symbols, and body gestures that can accelerate chakra activity. This sometimes confuses students of the chakra system, who assume that these mantras and symbols are ingrained in their chakra anatomy and are meant to be "found" there. However, whatever colorful visions these traditions offer—from a crocodile within the sacral chakra to Tibetan letters—these are mere tools for chakra enhancement.

The other group of practices, commonly associated with Western New Age culture, centers its attention on chakras as a system of psychological development. These practices suggest that through deep cognitive work on the chakras, we can energetically and spiritually transform them. For the purposes of this book, I highlight the psychological dimensions of the chakra system, reading it as an intricate blueprint of human needs, emotional evolution, life lessons, and personal forces. As useful indicators of the psychological process of maturation, each chakra advances through four main stages:

1. *Dysfunctional.* The individual feels too emotionally and mentally overwhelmed to respond to the challenges associated with the particular chakra and may even attempt to avoid these challenges.

2. *Functional.* Although the individual may be emotionally and mentally troubled, they are able to cope with chakra-related challenges.

3. *Balanced.* The individual has transformed the emotional and mental contents of the specific chakra, and when facing life situations that tend to provoke these contents, they remain calm and centered. This is a crucial stage in terms of psychological maturation, since a balanced chakra implies a profound inner wholeness and a sense of freedom from emotional dependency on the world around us.

4. *Awakened.* The individual has realized the deeper spiritual potential of the chakra and is able to experience its higher consciousness and qualities.

In a sense, the soul's journey can be understood as the journey toward the full activation of all seven chakras. By wholeheartedly responding to the complete range of challenges and life lessons contained within the chakras, one graduates from the school of life, as it were. Nevertheless, each chakra offers its own evolutionary path, representing particular dimensions of human growth. Since life highlights different dimensions at different times, the journey along the chakras is not necessarily linear, as you may imagine it to be. One day issues of the heart chakra may arise, and the following day your solar plexus chakra could move to the forefront. You should be able to identify phases of life in which you were either drawn to a specific chakra or compelled to cultivate its qualities and wisdom. This kind of periodical and ever-changing chakra development is guided by life's intelligent forces. But if you hope to deeply awaken all seven of your chakras in a traditional ladder-like progression, you will need to cultivate them energetically and psychologically in more conscious and proactive ways.

One last point that should be made in the context of this book is that, depending on the person, some chakras are felt more intensely than others for various reasons. This may result from a periodical focus on a certain chakra or triggers that either enhance or block one of your energy centers. This type of heightened awareness of a particular chakra should be distinguished from a far more fundamental reality of your subtle body. Bear in mind that some of your chakras are like your soul's center of gravity. As such, they naturally generate greater levels of energy, indicating that they are the centers of perception and experience that shape your personality and foster your individual soul's journey. These are your chakra types.

Chakra Basics

Chakra	Sanskrit name and meaning	Location	Element	Associated color	Seed mantra	Psychological aspects	Meditative state
Root chakra	Muladhara ("root" or "foundation")	Inside the perineum; corresponds to the legs and the skeletal and muscular systems	Earth	Red	Lam	Instinct, earthly and biological existence, security, groundedness, physical foundation and health, fear of instability and change, trauma	Inner stability
Sacral chakra	Svadhisthana ("one's dwelling place")	Lowest point of the spinal cord, at the level of the pubic bone; corresponds to the sex organs and the sacral plexus of nerves	Water	Orange/red	Vam	Feeling and impulse, vitality, adventure, totality, enjoyment, sensuality, pursuit of pleasure, sexuality, shame, the unconscious	Unconditional joy
Solar plexus chakra	Manipura ("city of jewels")	Behind the navel; corresponds to the digestive system and the solar plexus	Fire	Bright yellow	Ram	Willpower, individuality, independence, ambition, intensity, dynamism, courage, control, anger	True inner power; self-presence
Heart chakra	Anahata ("unstruck" or "unbeaten")	Behind the base of the heart, at the level of the depression in the sternum; corresponds to the cardiac plexus of nerves	Air	Blue	Yam	Emotions, relationships, love, attachment and dependency, betrayal and disappointment, forgiveness, letting go	Unconditional love; unity consciousness

Chakra Basics continued

Chakra	Sanskrit name and meaning	Location	Element	Associated color	Seed mantra	Psychological aspects	Medita-tive state
Throat chakra	Vishuddhi ("purity")	Behind the throat pit; corresponds to the cervical plexus of nerves	Ether	Violet	Ham	Communication, self-expression, lead-ership, manifestation, vision, authenticity, transparency	Boundless space
Brow chakra, also known as the third eye chakra or the guru chakra	Ajna ("command")	In the brain, behind the center of the eye-brows; corresponds to the pineal gland	Light	Silver/gray	Om	Intuition, intellect, clarity, insight, mental order, discrimination, attention, curiosity	Nondual perception
Crown chakra	Sahasrara ("one thousand")	Center of the top of the head, in the brain; corresponds to the pituitary gland	Cosmos; pure light and source of creation	Multicol-ored	Ah	Spirit, meditation, tran-scendence, timeless-ness, nonattachment, divine nature, univer-sality	Unlimited conscious-ness

Practice

· · · · · · ·

CHAKRA FLOWERING

Now that we have explored the theory of the chakra system together, I invite you to delve into the meditative practice known as "Chakra Flowering." This method provides an experiential understanding of the seven chakras, which will serve as a foundation for the subsequent detailed discussions of the chakra types.

The Chakra Flowering meditation is a transformative process that aids in stimulating and opening the chakras, allowing them to unfurl in their full bloom, reminiscent of a budding flower. An open flower is a fitting representation of an open chakra, for just as the flower sprouts from its stem, gradually revealing its beautiful, radiant petals, your chakras emerge from the central channel of your subtle body, progressing from the core to the front of your body, where they reach their ultimate state of bloom. Both an open chakra and an open flower are in an exposed, vulnerable state, willing to share their energy, beauty, and essence with the world, while also being receptive to nourishment and communication.

This meditation entails gradually moving upward from one chakra to another, visualizing each chakra's blossoming like a flower.

1. Settle into a comfortable posture. Gently close your eyes, take a deep breath, and relax your body with each breath cycle. Picture the fascinating diversity of the floral world, and envision a garden brimming with various types of flowers. See their vivid colors and smell their enchanting fragrances. For each of the chakras, you will intuitively choose a flower that serves as its perfect metaphor.

2. The central channel, the hidden place from which all chakras originate, is your starting point. To feel the presence of this channel, imagine a straight line passing through the center of your body, extending from just below your sexual organs to the top of your head.

3. Begin your exploration with the root chakra, nestled deep within the perineum, just beneath the sexual organs. It's vital to remember that the epicenter of this chakra, its inception point, resides in the central channel. The root chakra serves as the hub of your instinctual energies, your territorial awareness, and your senses of belonging and security. It is the anchor providing stability in your existence and protecting you. It represents the tranquility of feeling "at home" within your own physical form.

4. As you engage with the root chakra, imagine a flower coming into view. Visualize this chakra as a dormant flower bud, ready to awaken. As the blossom of the root chakra, this flower reaches downward, drawing sustenance from the earth and the elements of nature. As you inhale, gather the chakra's internal energies, and as you exhale, imagine these energies radiating outward from your body. Breathe life into this flower, and with each exhale, visualize it unfolding petal by petal. Experience the gradual unfurling of this flower from the central channel, reaching all the way down to the grounding energy of the earth.

5. Now, shift your focus to the sacral chakra. Situated just behind the pubic bone, at the apex of the sexual organs, the sacral chakra also finds its inception in the central channel. It's a whirlpool of joy, fervor, exhilaration, and the driving life force. It embodies the courage to venture into new opportunities, fostering an openness to truly feel and experience. Visualize a flower that represents this chakra slowly surfacing from the central stem. With each inhalation and exhalation, inspire this flower to gradually unfurl its petals, reaching full bloom.

6. Transition now to the solar plexus chakra. This power center is primarily nestled behind the navel, although its influence reaches to the solar plexus, just beneath the chest. You can sense the connection with this chakra, an abundant fountain of energy, ambition, resolve, and determination. This is the

chakra that fuels your inner strength, your unique identity, your capacity to confront adversity. Visualize a flower that embodies this chakra. As you breathe into this initially closed flower, gradually inspire it to open its petals. Continue until it radiates fully at the front of your body.

7. Shift your focus to the heart chakra. Positioned in the middle of the chest and nestled right at the bottom of the sternum, it resides deep within the central conduit of your body. This chakra is the center of relationships, emotions, and trust, and it has the potential to open you up to intimacy, unity, and even a sense of oneness. It also governs your capacity to extend care and empathy to others. Visualize a flower that serves as an embodiment of the heart chakra emerging from the stem within. As you breathe life into this flower, allow its sealed petals to unfurl gently, blooming fully at the center of your chest.

8. Transition your awareness to the throat chakra. It's situated in the lower-middle part of your neck, right behind the pit of the throat. Align yourself to this point along the central channel coursing through your body. The throat chakra stands as a beacon of manifestation and expression; it's the bridge that intertwines your inner and outer realms. This chakra plays a vital role in vocalizing and sharing your inner truth with the world around you. Envision a flower that perfectly epitomizes this chakra, and allow it to gradually develop and unfold through the rhythm of your breath, manifesting its full bloom at the front of your body.

9. Next, shift your focus to the third eye chakra, located within the brain, just slightly above the spot where your eyebrows converge. This chakra serves as the locus of insight, discerning vision, and comprehension of reality in its purest form. It allows you to perceive the subtler layers of existence with clarity. Envision a flower symbolizing this chakra. Then, let this blossom emerge from the depths of your brain until it flourishes fully across your forehead.

10. Finally, bring your consciousness to the crown chakra, nestled just beneath the apex of your head, within the brain. It's the termination of the central channel, the conclusion of the stem. This chakra is your bridge to the cosmos, transcending your personal boundaries and unveiling your luminous essence via profound meditation. Visualize a flower that represents this chakra, and inhale deeply into it. With each exhale, the flower starts to expand and unfurl, reaching full bloom to encompass the whole top of your head.

11. Now, sense the entire stem, stretching from the root chakra to the crown. Connect with the two terminal points of the stem and breathe life into this conduit, the source from which the entirety of your inner garden has blossomed. Allow your breath to flow through this channel, up and down, down and up.

12. With this newfound awareness of inner blossoming, gently allow your eyes to flutter open at your own pace.

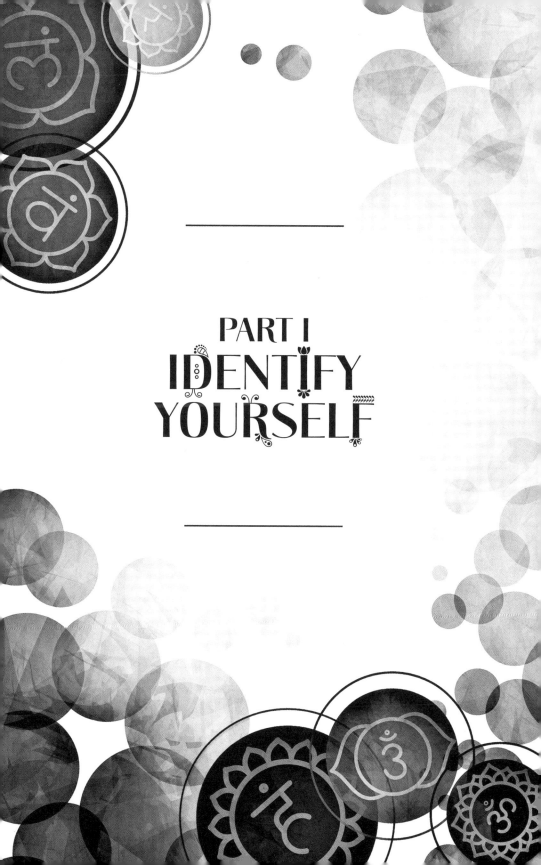

PART I
IDENTIFY YOURSELF

TWO

UNVEILING THE SEVEN PRIMARY TYPES

This chapter of the book is a comprehensive exploration of the seven primary chakra types, beginning with a detailed questionnaire designed to illuminate your personal chakra profile. Spanning twenty-five questions, each with seven distinct responses, this questionnaire is a tool to identify your dominant chakra energies, shaping your understanding of yourself as a unique blend of these powerful forces. Whether your answers resonate most with the Achiever, Builder, Caretaker, or another personality type, the pattern of your responses offers a first glance at your chakra constitution.

The latter half of the chapter unveils the fascinating universes of the seven primary chakra types. This section is crafted to introduce you to each primary chakra type, and also to guide you through the unique characteristics and perspectives associated with each chakra. As you engage with these descriptions, you are encouraged to reflect on how they align with your own life experiences, thereby enhancing your understanding of your dominant chakras. This chapter is a gateway to a more profound understanding of yourself, merging introspection with the ancient wisdom of chakra teachings and setting the stage for a transformative personal journey.

A Questionnaire: Sketching Your Soul Design

This questionnaire contains twenty-five questions. For each question, there are seven possible answers. You are invited to select one or two relevant answers to each question, though if you occasionally find yourself torn between three possible answers, it is fine to select three. The letters that you choose the most often may indicate your dominant chakras. Although your results may not be the complete picture of your chakra blueprint—as sometimes this process requires some rigorous soul-searching—the results will surely propel you in the right direction.

1. Select the statement you identify with the most.

   a. Life is an opportunity to build something solid—to diligently and patiently establish stability, groundedness, and peace of mind.

   b. The world is full of endless adventures and opportunities, and we are here to experience as many of them as possible.

   c. Life is an opportunity to bring out the best in ourselves, become a success story, and emerge victorious.

   d. The world is a space of emotional bonding, and we are here to real-ize our maximum potential as love in a human form.

   e. Life presents the opportunity to discover our message, express our truest voice, and influence others' lives.

   f. The world is a space of endless learning and knowledge, and our role in it is to stretch our intelligence and understanding as much as possible.

   g. Life is an opportunity for a profound inner journey of spiritual liberation and transcendence.

2. What would you say is the most active part of you?

   a. The earthly, grounded, and instinctual part of my being.

   b. My feelings, impulses, and the intelligence of my body.

   c. My willpower and ambition.

   d. My deep emotional world.

   e. My voice, expression, and communication.

f. My mind and intellect.

g. The spiritual part of my being.

3. Which imagery immediately makes you feel like you are in the right place?

a. A beautiful house, a garden, and prosperous land.

b. Someone dancing in a trancelike, ecstatic state at a party.

c. Climbing a mountaintop, nearly reaching the peak.

d. Two people's hands entwining and caressing each other.

e. A speaker in a big lecture hall facing a large crowd.

f. A library and a lone writer sitting in it, immersed in their own world.

g. A monk in deep meditation.

4. My ideal way of sharing my being with others is…

a. Serving the needs of my family and community with my skills and abilities.

b. Having fun, laughing, dancing, and experiencing physical and sensual joy.

c. Striving toward some shared target with effort and determination.

d. A one-on-one, personal, and intimate sharing in which we open our hearts to one another.

e. Guiding others or discussing and creating a grand vision with them.

f. Engaging in a profound philosophical discussion with a thoughtful person.

g. Meditating, praying, and simply being with others who are spiritually oriented.

5. The best way I could spend my time is by…

a. Carrying out small actions and plans that put life into order and balance.

b. Immersing myself in the outdoors, moving my body, and breathing the moment deep into my being.

    c. Making sure that everything I do can lead me to my goal.

    d. Helping someone and making sure they are happy.

    e. Writing or recording a message that could change people's lives.

    f. Delving into a book by a great philosopher.

    g. Watching a video of a spiritual or religious teacher.

6. Since childhood, my main connection with the world has been through…

    a. My search for belonging and my role in the systems of the world.

    b. Playfulness and experimentation.

    c. Winning in various competitions and other settings.

    d. Strong feelings toward certain others.

    e. Educating and leading others.

    f. Distant observation and quiet inner study.

    g. Indifference and unbelonging.

7. Others would say that I am…

    a. Diligent, serious, responsible, cautious, and accurate.

    b. Restless, intense, passionate, humorous, and always hunting for a new experience.

    c. Ambitious, driven, focused, busy, and competitive.

    d. Emotional, sensitive, caring, helpful, and kindhearted.

    e. Inquisitive, controlling, intense, idealistic, and expressive.

    f. Wise, silent, distant, deep, and aware.

    g. Spiritual, introverted, unearthly, gentle, and dreamy.

8. At heart, I am a…

    a. Hard worker.

    b. Dancer.

    c. Warrior.

    d. Lover.

    e. Communicator.

    f. Philosopher.

    g. Meditator.

9. I am…

    a. Slow and careful.

    b. Quick and spontaneous.

    c. Persistent and determined.

    d. Mild and harmonious.

    e. Intense and engaging.

    f. Distant and observant.

    g. Dreamy and spacey.

10. Choose the word that you respond the most to.

    a. Foundation.

    b. Passion.

    c. Victory.

    d. Love.

    e. Vision.

    f. Wisdom.

    g. Silence.

11. Which building sounds the most interesting and impressive to you?

    a. An ancient history museum.

    b. A whimsical, artistic building.

    c. A skyscraper.

    d. A sanctuary for the underserved.

    e. A congressional hall.

    f. A university.

    g. An ashram or a monastery.

12. When I leave this world, I want to know that…

    a. I have benefited and contributed to my family, community, and people.

    b. I have experienced life totally and let it in fully.

    c. I have achieved the highest goals I set for myself.

    d. I have loved strongly enough.

e. I have left behind a legacy of influence and impact.

f. I have understood some of life's hidden mysteries.

g. I have experienced my innermost spirit.

13. Which of these negative attributes characterizes you the most?

a. Overcaution.

b. Lack of commitment.

c. Anger.

d. Neediness.

e. A controlling nature.

f. Arrogance.

g. Detachment.

14. How do you feel when you read the following statement? "I love dealing with details—calculations and figures, materials and accurate planning, pieces of information, and schedules."

a. Yes! I totally agree.

b. No, dealing with details makes me want to fly away. I love doing nothing!

c. Yes, but only if it leads me to some clear and powerful goal.

d. Yes, but only if it clearly helps me serve someone I love.

e. No, I would rather leap to the vision at the edge of my imagination.

f. No, small details have no intelligence or depth in them.

g. No, earthly life has no spiritual meaning.

15. When an overwhelming negative emotion arises in me, I...

a. Do anything I can to calm it down and put myself back together.

b. Become one with it, totally experience it, and quickly return to joy.

c. Take it out on my surroundings.

d. Become overwhelmed and struggle to transform it into harmony.

e. Try to control and suffocate it.

f. Investigate it as a scientist.

g. Meditate.

16. How much do you like change and mobility in life (as opposed to routine and permanence)?
    a. Big changes feel unhealthy and destabilizing for me. I prefer slow and gradual change.
    b. Change is my middle name. I always feel on fire and can't stand routine!
    c. I don't like disruptions, but I know how to adjust them to my plans.
    d. I am fine with changes as long as I get to keep all my loved ones with me.
    e. I get confused when things change and collide with the dream inside me.
    f. I prefer to create a routine that allows me to deeply explore the mental realm.
    g. I don't initiate changes, but I can accept changes when they come as God's will.

17. How would you describe your type and level of energy?
    a. Slow and persistent, like a low flame.
    b. Rapid, quick, and physical, like a flare.
    c. Massive and uncompromising, like a bulldozer.
    d. Gentle and soft, like a breeze.
    e. Intense and wakeful.
    f. Mainly concentrated in my head, not so physical.
    g. Airy, like levitation.

18. I feel most alive when…
    a. I manage to grasp the inner mechanism of something.
    b. I am experiencing creative expression.
    c. I manage to remove obstacles and take a step forward.
    d. I am in a state of intimacy and bonding.
    e. I manage to influence and affect the lives of others.
    f. I have new and brilliant insights.
    g. I manage to enter deep states of consciousness.

19. How do you feel when you read the following statement? "I want to change the world!"

    a. My aspirations are not that great. However, I want to know that I have benefited others and my community.

    b. Far from it. I just want to be myself and express that creatively and authentically.

    c. I want to conquer the world!

    d. I just spread love with all my heart. Whatever happens, happens.

    e. Yes—by spreading my ideas, visions, and creations, I dream of having a global impact.

    f. My thoughts and ideas are far too deep to change the common people.

    g. Global change is none of my concern. I am only occupied with the eternal.

20. Think of the color that best represents your deepest, innermost being (as opposed to your "favorite" color). Which of the following colors most closely resembles the color of your inner being?

    a. Deep red.

    b. Fizzy orange.

    c. Radiant yellow.

    d. Soft and light green.

    e. Deep and intense blue.

    f. Lush and mysterious purple.

    g. Bright white; colorless.

21. Choose your most cherished values.

    a. Respect, loyalty, patience.

    b. Joy, totality, beauty.

    c. Courage, perseverance, dignity.

    d. Compassion, friendship, harmony.

    e. Authenticity, autonomy, self-expression.

    f. Intelligence, clarity, depth.

    g. Purity, nonattachment, freedom.

22. How do you feel when you read the following statement? "I love being part of a larger unit like a tradition, family, community, or nation. It feels healthy and supportive."

    a. Perfectly accurate.

    b. Not at all! I avoid frameworks that limit my freedom of choice and experience.

    c. I appreciate structures, but it is most important for me to stand out and be myself.

    d. Structures are wonderful as long as they are opportunities for love.

    e. I am more interested in my dreams about better, even utopian, communities.

    f. Such structures are for common people. I prefer to research this phenomenon.

    g. Only if these larger units are spiritual and support spirituality.

23. How much do you like long-term projects and lifetime commitments?

    a. A lot—as long as they are relaxed and secure processes.

    b. The very idea terrifies me. I feel like I'm in a cage.

    c. I like them as long as they lead to some successful end and are constantly growing and expanding.

    d. I like them, but they need to be essentially emotional commitments.

    e. I like them, but only if they include a vision that thrills me and never stifles my dreams.

    f. I like them if they are intellectual by nature and lead to new depths.

    g. My only lifelong commitment is to my spiritual journey.

24. Choose the figure that you relate to the most.

    a. Thomas Edison, inventor.

    b. Jim Morrison, rock legend and poet.

    c. Ernesto "Che" Guevara, warrior and revolutionary.

    d. Mother Teresa, missionary of charity.

    e. Martin Luther King Jr., speaker and leader.

    f. Sigmund Freud, psychologist and theorist.

    g. Francis of Assisi, saint.

25. Which historical revolution impresses you the most?

   a. The agricultural or industrial revolution.

   b. The social revolution of the '60s (the flower children).

   c. The victory in the Second World War.

   d. Nonviolent peace movements like Gandhi's and King's.

   e. The emergence of democracy in ancient Athens.

   f. Ancient Greek philosophy.

   g. The emergence of teachers like the Buddha or Jesus.

TOTALS:

a: _____ b: _____ c: _____ d: _____ e: _____ f: _____ g: _____

Decoding Your Chakra Types from Quiz Responses

After determining the three letters you selected most in your questionnaire, translate these into their matching chakra types:

- Mostly As: Root chakra type (Builder)
- Mostly Bs: Sacral chakra type (Artist)
- Mostly Cs: Solar plexus chakra type (Achiever)
- Mostly Ds: Heart chakra type (Caretaker)
- Mostly Es: Throat chakra type (Speaker)
- Mostly Fs: Third eye chakra type (Thinker)
- Mostly Gs: Crown chakra type (Yogi)

Next, reflect on the letter that was your runner-up, as it may represent your secondary chakra type. Finally, the letter in the third place may provide insight into your supportive chakra type. For instance, if you selected answer C fifteen times, answer A ten times, and answer D nine times, your dominant chakra types would be the solar plexus, the root, and the heart. Thus, for the sake of this questionnaire, you would be a solar plexus chakra type, an Achiever, with a secondary Builder type and a supportive Caretaker type.

Preparing for Your Self-Exploration

As you embark on this deep dive into the seven primary chakras, it's important to read about all seven chakra types—do not just focus on the dominant types you identified and skip the rest. Also, have a notepad or digital device ready. Following the detailed exploration of each chakra, pause and take a moment to truthfully evaluate how closely your life experiences align with the descriptions provided. This measurement can range anywhere from 0 percent to 100 percent.

In certain instances, a chakra profile might seem to echo only a sliver of your being—perhaps a mere 10 percent. It is highly unlikely for anyone to score a clean zero, given that each of us embodies aspects of all seven chakras. Other descriptions may resonate more significantly, somewhere between 30 percent to 40 percent. While some individuals may feel compelled to provide astonishingly precise scores, like 37.5 percent, there is no need for such accuracy—whole numbers from 10 to 100 will do.

At times, a chakra profile may resonate with you so deeply that it feels like it is 100 percent representative of you. This doesn't mean that every facet of the description will align perfectly. Rather, it may feel like you are reading a reflection of yourself. Naturally, if you rank a chakra profile as 100 percent compatible, you have likely found your primary chakra type, barring the unusual scenario in which another profile also earns a 100 percent score from you. It's not uncommon to be torn between two leading chakras, which is completely normal at this stage.

You might be curious why I recommended using percentages to understand the specific roles of the three dominant chakras. This system is effective because it shows how closely each chakra is connected to the soul's core. The highest percentage indicates that chakra is very important to the soul's journey. The chakra with the second-highest percentage will help you express your inner nature, and the third-highest percentage represents the chakra that plays a supporting role. Think of it as a target with rings—the closer a chakra is to the center, the more it influences your being. Chakras with lower percentages act more like tools; they are assisting you, but they don't define your core essence. Essentially, tools are things you use, while your essence is what fundamentally defines you.

Even after you have filled out the initial questionnaire, it is valuable to approach the descriptions of the chakra types anew, allowing for a more lucid and profound understanding of each type's essence. You may stumble upon subtle yet significant insights that you hadn't noticed before. These nuances hold a particular importance when you are still uncertain about your primary chakra type or when deciding if a certain type serves as your primary or secondary chakra. Thus, by the end of part I, you should be able to identify the three dominant chakras in your blueprint. Combined with the insights from the questionnaire and the upcoming exercises in chapter 3, the intricate mosaic of your soul will slowly, surely come to light.

Each of the following descriptions was written to answer nine fundamental questions. (You'll find these questions explained in more detail, and in order, in chapter 5.) My process always begins with a general exploration of each chakra's central elements. As mentioned in the introduction, my approach to developing this system was rooted in meditative contemplation, visualizing how a distinct personality would emerge from a specific chakra. I immersed myself in the themes associated with each chakra, envisioning them taking human form. I have outlined the distinct personalities that evolved directly from these thematic foundations. I also delve into the nuances of life experiences, including the quest for purpose, happiness, and fulfillment that resonates with each personality type. Moreover, I'll address the strengths and potential pitfalls of each chakra type, the elemental narrative that encapsulates the fundamental conflict or challenge one may grapple with in life, and strategies to harmonize this tension. Lastly, I illuminate how each chakra behaves when it plays a secondary or supportive role in your life. Even though this seems comprehensive, I have not provided exhaustive descriptions. It would be possible to dedicate an entire chapter to each chakra type, so I have chosen to concentrate on the key aspects necessary for you to discern each type's presence within your personal blueprint.

Though not grounded in precise scientific statistics, I want to provide a rough division of the seven primary chakra types across the global population. A significant portion—around 40 percent—identifies with the root chakra type (Builder), while 25 percent align with the solar plexus chakra type (Achiever), together making up 65 percent of the global populace. Another prevalent type, vital for a thriving society, is the heart chakra type (Caretaker), accounting for approximately 15 percent of the population. Together, these groups represent 80 percent of humanity. The remaining chakra types are distributed across smaller demographics: the throat chakra types (the Speakers), while constituting only 7 percent of the population, have a particularly prominent presence as they often assume leadership roles in the world. The sacral chakra type (Artist) also represents a mere 7 percent. Even more scarce, the third eye chakra types (the Thinkers) comprise no more than 5 percent, while the crown chakra types (the Yogis) are a rare breed, making up a mere 1 percent of the population.

Again, this isn't based on science but more on how I imagine the balance of different types of people in the world. Interestingly, I once asked sixty participants in a chakra types course to share their three-type structure. We used this info to create a population divide chart. The results confirmed my estimates. I offer these estimates to inspire a snapshot of what a fully functioning society, balanced among the seven types, might resemble.

The following sections adhere to the classical approach of starting at the base of the central channel and gradually ascending the chakra hierarchy. Therefore, I initially outline the first three chakra types—the root, the sacral, and the solar plexus—which all share a significant characteristic. Specifically, in the context of their chakra construction, they constitute a three-chakra sequence intimately connected to the physical and terrestrial realm.

The Material-Earthly Types
(Builders, Artists, and Achievers)

These three chakra types hold a fervent interest in particular aspects of tangible, worldly life experiences. Their curiosity veers away from the abstract and toward the concrete elements of life, which captivate them immensely. Nonetheless, what specifically enchants them varies significantly among these types.

The Root Chakra Type (Builders)

This is the most frequently encountered chakra type. It's crucial to note that "most frequent" doesn't imply "less vital"—in fact, it suggests the opposite. Builders, in their truest essence, are the architects of the world. They lay the groundwork and ensure the seamless operation and growth of the world's systems. Therefore, theirs is an immense responsibility. Much of the world as we know it has been shaped by the efforts of Builders.

Let's embark on this journey by tapping into the root chakra. Recall that it's situated at the base of the spine, deep within the perineum region, branching out to the legs and knees. It's not only a regulator for the skeletal and muscular systems but also serves as the bedrock supporting the entire body's structure. Given its association with the legs, this chakra influences how we metaphorically take a stand and plant our feet firmly on life's path. As you tune in to this chakra, consider its areas of focus, which include survival, instinct, and security, as well as relationships with the tangible physical world. The root chakra also encompasses health and physical nourishment. It extends its influence to kinship and blood relations, reaching out to primary connections shared with parents, children, the community, and territory. When contemplating the root chakra, a critical term that resonates is *home*—home not only as a physical shelter, but also the sensation of belonging and feeling at home. Therefore, when the root chakra is imbalanced, we may enter a state of unease and distress, as we are disoriented within our own being and our position in the world.

Personality Traits

So, what personality traits manifest from these themes? Imagine the root chakra type as the one most energetically and even geographically—owing to its proximity—linked to the earth. This implies that it's the personality that interacts most directly with the earth's laws and the principles of matter. Consequently, it encapsulates the wisdom and intellect of the physical world, along with the body's intelligence. Builders instinctively grasp the physical and material dimension, as if they possess an innate understanding of them. Thus, they are intuitively linked to the laws of matter. But what does this mean? Consider, for instance, the rules that trigger a flower's blooming process. Root chakra personalities often gravitate toward occupations like farming due to how captivating they find the laws of matter. They usually relish nurturing plants, finding joy in the observation of an intelligent pattern: growth when water is provided. They revere the earth's wisdom, nature's intelligent cycles and seasons, and the intricate design by which the body operates.

Yet the allure of the root chakra type isn't confined to nature, earth, and the physical form; it extends to anything governed by law, such as the operation of machines due to mechanical principles. This personality type often finds joy in machinery, architectural design, the healing properties of medicine and herbs, and even the establishment of orderly societies through legislation. All of these fall under the umbrella of functioning systems. This embrace extends to traditions and heritages, as there's an inherent beauty in a system that continually evolves yet has remained preserved over millennia. Consequently, Builders exhibit a deep reverence for the past, underpinned by a profound understanding of evolution—how entities evolved gradually over millions or even billions of years, and how cultures have blossomed steadily yet securely.

Imagine this chakra type as one that instinctively aligns with a cosmic sense of order and law. This is why their creed could be "God is in the details," as they see divinity realized in the intelligence orchestrating everything from flowers blooming to the most fundamental laws of nature, which might seem trivial yet are crucial to the world's stability. Guided by this understanding of law and order, Builders ceaselessly aspire to increased balance and harmony. If two phrases could encapsulate the essence of the root chakra type, they would be "devotion to balance" and "fondness for harmony."

They delight in maintaining equilibrium and peace, ensuring a smooth, controlled flow in all aspects of life. This preference is due to their intuitive grasp of the wisdom and order underlying the physical world. They strive to uncover the "how," the mechanics of systems (such as bodily functions), and then apply this knowledge to enhance these systems; for instance, striving for consistent health or overall wellness. Hence, Builders are committed to systemic refinement in the pursuit of greater harmony and balance. They display an exceptional level of patience, thinking predominantly in terms of long-term system cultivation and gradual progression. This explains why they are called Builders! Every Builder knows that to construct a house, a robust infrastructure is a prerequisite, and every detail must be meticulously planned—otherwise, everything risks collapse.

As previously mentioned, individuals embodying the root chakra type can be found amongst farmers and architects, but their presence extends far and wide. Their diverse occupations may include medical professionals who marvel at the intricacies of anatomy and physiology, surgeons driven by a fascination with the inner workings and enhancement of organ function, or laboratory researchers who relish the opportunity to explore minutiae through the lens of a microscope. Builders can also be drawn to the realm of law and order, working as law enforcement officers, accountants, lawyers (particularly those who appreciate the meticulous nuances of the law), and judges. For example, an accountant with a primary root chakra type experiences genuine excitement when engaging with numbers, as they find solace and assurance in the consistent outcomes that numbers, mathematics, and the laws of the physical world provide. Furthermore, Builders' affinity for maintaining order and ensuring seamless operations make them well suited for positions as secretaries and administrative managers, taking painstaking care of schedules and effectively managing time. Another facet of this personality may manifest within religious communities, where priests and other devout individuals embody the traits associated with the root chakra.

When you inquire about the core values of a root chakra type, their responses often revolve around two crucial aspects: family and home. These individuals prioritize their families and reliably fulfill familial responsibilities. Furthermore, the significance of having a place to call their own cannot be understated, as it provides them with a profound sense of grounding. While their personal abode serves as their foundation, they also hold a deep appreciation for contributing to the community. They actively engage in community activities and take pride in being part of a larger society, valuing its efficient functioning. Their life's purpose derives from their ability to enhance systems, instilling order, law, and harmony within them. Whether it is an office, family life, a residential dwelling, a commercial establishment, or even a farm, Builders strive to bring improvements and find meaning in such endeavors. They are driven by their passion to bring the order they see in their minds into the material world.

Looking at the merits of the root chakra type, their inherently peaceful disposition stands out. They prefer a quiet, tranquil life and avoid conflicts and disagreements as much as they can—unless their understanding of law and order is severely challenged, in which case they become anxious and might even raise their voice. As a rule, Builders display immense patience. Likened to the nurturing gardeners of life, they are faithful, reliable, and systematic. Their aptitude for appreciating small details and adeptly managing them is commendable, as this is something that other chakra types may struggle with. You can often spot a root chakra type when someone around you seems to relish the time spent deciphering how things work, including the technical nuances of newly purchased gadgets.

However, this love for detail also stems from anxiety and insecurity. Builders adhere to this type of order because it assures them of a stable world. This brings us to the root chakra type's weaknesses. Their constant desire for everything to stay orderly, balanced, and harmonious often leads to anxiety and worry, especially since life can be unpredictable and other chakra types tend to be messier. As a result, Builders might live in a perpetual state of unease and concern.

Builders also form strong attachments to their possessions and people, to the point of possessiveness. Their fear of loss (in terms of death, disaster, and other drastic change) underpins this behavior. They are profoundly territorial, desiring control over their space and making every effort to protect it from encroachment. They often exhibit excessive calculation, and when it comes to financial matters, they typically harbor a fear of risks.

Generally, Builders are highly resistant to change, making them somewhat traditional and quick to dismiss new ideas. If you introduce something utterly new, revolutionary, and life-altering, their initial reaction will probably be "No, this can't be real." This doesn't mean they will never adopt a new technology or system, but they will take a lot longer than others to do so. They would prefer to wait and see if others accept it first. If the innovation becomes mainstream and it clearly doesn't cause disruption, Builders will then say, "Okay, it seems safe to incorporate this into the world." In this sense, they can be slow, not only physically but also in their thought process. They need time to absorb and understand new information; they can't handle a fast-paced, demanding environment.

This leads Builders to form an intense attachment to routine, to such an extent that they could practically repeat the same day forever. Naturally, other chakra types might perceive them as hopelessly monotonous, and their lives can indeed be somewhat colorless and bland. They don't seek a life brimming with excitement. You wouldn't approach a root chakra type for the latest news because, to them, nothing is new, and they are content with that. An old Chinese saying is "May you live in interesting times," which is actually a curse, especially for a Builder! The root chakra type doesn't seek an interesting life. They also lack a sense of humor. This doesn't mean they can't laugh, but they aren't naturally funny, and they don't perceive the world in a humorous or ironic way.

These prevailing dispositions ultimately lead to the core struggle of the root chakra type: a profound aversion to change. These individuals deeply hope life will remain static and unchanging. This might seem odd, since Builders certainly value the principles underlying the physical world. So why, then, would they dismiss the most inherent attribute of the physical world— constant evolution? Change is an integral part of the natural order of life, encompassing phenomena like sicknesses, accidents, death, chaos, upheavals, and abrupt alterations to life such as divorce or job loss. Yet, the root chakra type would prefer to omit this chapter from the book of life. They see life as an unalterable reality, and this perspective explains why their most profound traumas are linked to abrupt changes that cause their world to spin out of control, hastening the pace of life and leaving them reeling, robbed of familiar truths.

In the obscured sections of their psyche, Builders aspire to halt life's progression. They seek to govern it, to evade risks so effectively that nothing unpredictable can possibly occur. However, as life refuses to accept their terms, root chakra types subconsciously develop a sense of defiance, adopting the mindset of "If you, life, refuse to remain constant, I shall remain unchanging." As a result, they craft a small, unchangeable sanctuary, a place that they believe life's transformations can't penetrate. In doing so, they somewhat stifle their vibrancy, repeating the same day indefinitely, all in the pursuit of asserting their victory in this lifelong struggle.

So, how does the root chakra type resolve these innate tensions? The first step is to accept their nature, as it is with all chakra types. This doesn't mean that Builders should become a tempest of excitement, vibrancy, and speed; they play an essential role in the world by merely existing as they are. However, they must also recognize life's ever-evolving nature and understand that the dimension to which they are intimately connected (the rhythm of natural cycles) inherently involves change and evolution. In simpler terms, harmonious coexistence with life involves flowing with life's current rather than standing against it. This mirrors Taoist teachings about learning to adapt to change and softening rigid perspectives. Builders could benefit significantly from therapeutic practices to find equilibrium amid life's sudden shifts. Furthermore, they need to periodically disrupt their routines and challenge themselves. Otherwise, life will invariably do it for them!

The Secondary Root Chakra Type

For those who have the root chakra as their secondary chakra type, this suggests that their constitution is deeply grounded, with their fulfillment anchored in stability. The secondary root chakra type translates the primary chakra type's essence into various forms and life structures. For instance, if a heart chakra type had a secondary root chakra, they would be inclined to channel their strong feelings of love, compassion, and care into creating structures for others, for example by building a home for the unhoused or starting a philanthropic foundation. Motivated by their vision of love, they would strive to create a conduit for its fulfillment. Thus, the secondary root chakra centralizes its fulfillment on creating systems of harmony and balance and finding solutions to help others manage life structures, like time management or physical well-being. A secondary root chakra also increases one's focus on community contributions.

The Supportive Root Chakra Type

For those with a supportive root chakra type, it becomes a source of nourishment and empowerment. Therefore, connections with family, routine, and maintaining a balanced lifestyle become their anchors. This implies that they draw energy from this type of stable foundation. It's not only a deep necessity but also a source of strength; simply knowing that they have this stability can propel them forward.

Collecting Your Thoughts

Pause and absorb the information you've just read. Intuitively estimate what percentage of this chakra type constitutes your profound life experience. Remember, your complete soul design comprises three chakra types, so no one is expected to entirely or disproportionately embody the root chakra personality. In my own soul design, the root chakra type makes up only 10 percent; I'm curious about your percentage.

The Sacral Chakra Type (Artists)

Before exploring the complexities of the sacral chakra, allow yourself a moment to locate and connect with this energy center within your own body. Imagine it situated just beyond your pubic bone, in the upper part of your genital area. It is a potent locus positioned deep beneath the navel, reaching out to encompass both your sexual organs and kidneys. The issues tethered to this chakra greatly influence your zest for life, how vivacious and eager you feel—or, alternatively, how desolate and depressed you may become.

In the context of the chakra system, the sacral chakra is directly linked to your feelings. Unlike emotions, feelings are tied to your most intuitive experiences of life, i.e., everything that you encounter directly. For instance, when you engage with a flower, you might be filled with an overwhelming sense of joy. This joy is a testament to your bond with life and even represents a form of unity with it. Through this effervescent delight, you form a unique closeness with the flower. Thus, feelings illustrate the intensity of your inner life force, reflecting how alive, ecstatic, invigorated, joyful, and passionate you feel about life and the present moment. On the opposite end of the spectrum, feelings can also manifest as depression, loss of enthusiasm, apathy, indifference, and even exhaustion, embodying fatigue and a refusal to engage with life. Hence, while emotions are the threads that either bind or separate us in relationships, feelings encapsulate a direct connection to life within and around us.

Your capacity to experience profound, intense, and passionate feelings is directly influenced by your sacral chakra. Another key attribute of this chakra is impulse: your ability to spontaneously act upon sudden desires. This places the sacral chakra at the epicenter of many subconscious motifs, as it directly engages with taboo desires and temptations and the dichotomy of what's forbidden and permitted, which inevitably encompasses sexual expression. Furthermore, the sacral chakra dictates your adventurous spirit, courage, and willingness to fully immerse yourself in an experience, including how much pleasure you permit yourself to feel. This chakra also governs physical movement and the ability to find joy in it. As the chakra of the senses, it asks you to consider how open your senses truly are. As a result, it also touches upon the theme of aesthetics via sensitivity to beauty and an ability to appreciate and derive pleasure from the beautiful aspects of life.

Personality Traits

Picture now the character that takes shape from these traits, a character that starkly contrasts with the root chakra type's yearning for stability. The sacral chakra type is an Artist, not by occupation, but by virtue of their artistic soul. They view life as a divine canvas, a blend of energies and hues. The sacral chakra type is gifted with the intelligence of feeling and sensation; thus, they experience things profoundly. Artists are beings who enter this world radiating life. To an extent, they are restless, as they struggle to contain the vibrant life force that pulsates within them. They live with this internal outburst, akin to a flare. This inner blaze propels them forward, but it also frequently compels them to disengage from situations when the spark dims. They might say, "I don't wish to remain here. This isn't exciting anymore. I don't feel the flame within me."

Artists primarily navigate their lives guided by urges, feelings, and sensory perceptions. Living life governed by such impulses resembles being a butterfly flitting from one flower to the next, driven by an insatiable desire to experience everything. Another aspect of being driven by urges and sensory perceptions is that Artists engage with the world bodily; this is how they experience everything. This perception of the body is distinct from the root chakra type's view. Builders desire to preserve the body as a stronghold of health and stability, rooted in the wisdom of structure. Artists, conversely, perceive through the body, using it as a means to affirm their truths. If the body responds with joy and enthusiasm, they take it as confirmation of their truth!

This archetype enters the world with an innate bond with nature, purely because they are an extension of nature itself. They are a living manifestation of life force. Moreover, Artists perpetually seek the enchanting elements of life, as they perceive life itself to be a wonder, and therefore inherently magical. In this context, they also possess a deep poetic sensibility. They may not pen verses, but they feel like poets at heart. This is how they engage with the world, in pursuit of magic and enchanted moments. They aim to capture fleeting sentiments.

Artists perceive life as a tapestry of energies. Life, for them, is a celebration, or even a game devoid of any concrete purpose. Why does life exist? Merely because it's an enthralling play. They are ardent admirers of life in its raw form. Consequently, they strive to connect with the present moment, often with little regard for future aspirations. They fail to comprehend the significance of long-term plans, arguing that such planning overlooks life's fundamental essence. They doubt the logic of constructing so much in life when its transitory nature suggests that it's more valuable to invest in what is right in front of them. Artists are not creatures of the past either; they swiftly let go of previous happenings, as they don't hold on to long-term memories of experiences. For them, life's authenticity is in the here and now.

Artists, in many ways, embody a sense of anarchy. Given the chance to shape the world, those with a primary sacral chakra might not construct grand infrastructures. Instead, they envision a world where people play freely, basking in rivers and lakes, engaging in music, and dancing around bonfires. This is their ideal society. Perceiving the world through this lens, Artists often question why others take life so seriously. To them, the persistent earnestness of "grown-ups" is perplexing: What is it that these somber folks are constantly preoccupied with? What is their ultimate goal?

From the Artist's standpoint, the true meaning of life is to have complete and immersive experiences—chances to come into contact with life in a tangible, sensuous manner through physical sensations, the feeling of touch, various aromas, and the beauty of sight. Artists are naturally intertwined with life through the vital energy that courses through their own bodies, and they detect that energy in every aspect of existence. They are passionately committed to unlocking the potential of sensory experiences. Their happiest moments occur during peak experiences—special, exciting events that make them feel their strongest. They also cherish moments when they feel unlimited and free, with nothing holding them back.

Individuals with a primary sacral chakra can be found in a variety of roles, working as tantra instructors, guides for shamanic or emotional journeys, physical catharsis coaches, or even tour guides. They also find their place among artists such as photographers, poets, painters, musicians, and comedians. In fact, we owe humor largely to sacral chakra types! As connoisseurs of fine taste and good food, they may also emerge as chefs, winemakers, or wine tasters. In culinary roles, they are known for their exceptional creativity, always seeking to innovate rather than reiterate the same dishes, unlike their more "conventional" counterparts. Occasionally, Artists transition into entrepreneurship, brimming with novel and exhilarating ideas.

Among the defining strengths of Artists, their profound independence and unbridled spirit stand out. They are typically bursting with a zest for life, but occasionally, they might deviate from this innate joy for several reasons, including having contradictory chakra types in their internal spectrum. They generally have a rich sense of humor and exude an irresistible charm. In individual encounters, Artists make others feel as if they are the only person in the world, yet the Artist swiftly moves on, leaving individuals bewildered and emotionally bruised. The Artist frolics onward, seemingly oblivious to their past connection (though they might hold on to pleasant shared moments). Thus, sacral chakra types truly embody totality, as they have an intense capacity to feel and experience. Their depth of feeling remains unmatched by other chakra types. Artists are also highly attuned to beauty and generally possess a refined taste. If someone needs advice on interior decor, the Artist instinctively knows where everything belongs because they have an inherent sense for aesthetics. Their sensory experiences are incredibly raw and vulnerable, leading to an intense perception of touch. They have an adventurous spirit and love for change.

Among the challenges often associated with the sacral chakra type, their tendency to defy stands out—though they themselves may not see this as a weakness. They have a strong attraction to forbidden actions; if you tell them not to do something, their response is likely to be, "That's exactly what I'll do!" Their rebellious nature and aversion to structured environments can cause issues, particularly in corporate settings with established rules and regulations. Their disinclination for long-term commitments can also make them seem unreliable; they may forget a promise as quickly as they made it due to their fluctuating excitement levels. As a result, they can come across as self-centered, primarily focused on their own feelings and interests. Not only do they tend to think mostly about themselves, but they also tend to monopolize conversations. Furthermore, Artists often resist the responsibilities of adulthood, which can manifest as laziness. They prefer to live life to the fullest while exerting the least possible effort. Their love for change often leads to a lack of routine and a disordered lifestyle. Lastly, due to their relentless pursuit of excitement and a "high," Artists may be prone to developing dependencies on certain substances or experiences.

The sacral chakra type's narrative revolves around their deep-seated craving for freedom. This profound need can lead them to resist commitment and complete devotion. Paradoxically, they also seek the depth of experience that only commitment can bring. They grapple with the understanding that life's full potential only unveils itself when one commits to people, tasks, and selfless actions. However, Artists typically avoid discomfort and strenuous effort. Consequently, they tend to skim across life's surface, relishing experiences but rarely delving into profound contrasts like pain and joy. They perceive commitment as a form of finality and pain as an experience to be negated and repressed. In their essential narrative, they strive to straddle two worlds: preserving their childlike innocence while attempting to shoulder adult responsibilities. This contradictory combination often proves unsuccessful, but confronting this challenge is an adult task they'd rather sidestep.

Artists can attain equilibrium by acknowledging their unique value system. Living in a world dominated by Builders (associated with the first chakra), Achievers (related to the third chakra), and Caretakers (linked to the fourth chakra) can be challenging. Artists must understand that while their value system may be unconventional, it holds great significance and beauty. At the same time, they need to recognize that life has values beyond mere experience and strive to harmonize the concepts of lightness and depth. In this context, they would benefit from seeking environments that allow them to encapsulate both elements simultaneously. For instance, a company that provides a conducive space for creativity without excessive pressure could enable them to be committed while preserving their free spirit.

The Secondary Sacral Chakra Type

As a secondary chakra type, the Artist has an ungrounded inner nature. Fulfillment is tied to a bubbling, eruptive force. This means life should be flexible and not follow a strict routine. Interactions, tasks, and sharing their talents will be short-lived. They often move quickly from one activity to another, always in motion. To truly thrive, they need to live a life that isn't tied down to one thing. This often involves helping others find joy, which might include teaching physical movement, sacred sexuality, or how to connect with nature.

The Supportive Sacral Chakra Type

When the sacral chakra is the supportive chakra type, power and sustenance stem from a bond with nature and the pursuit of pleasure, physical activity, and movement. Activities like dancing every day, even briefly, could recharge them. A life full of change, free from absolute order and rigid routines, also supports them. When this chakra personality acts as the supportive type, acknowledging these needs is crucial, or they might feel drained. Regardless of their primary and secondary types, a supportive sacral chakra is an individual's power source.

Collecting Your Thoughts

Now, pause and attune yourself to the essence of this chakra type. To what extent do you identify with the Artist within you?

The Solar Plexus Chakra Type (Achievers)

Begin by centering your attention on this radiant chakra. It possesses two epicenters: one located slightly behind the navel and the other in the solar plexus region, below the chest, which is often more palpably sensed. Spend a moment connecting with this upper abdominal region that regulates the digestive system.

The challenges tied to the solar plexus mainly involve the idea of power—specifically, how much power you think you have. It also deals with the sense of self: Are you a strong individual? Do you know when and how to say "no"? How can you gather and unify your will to achieve your goals? Can you use your resources to overcome problems, whether facing challenges from within yourself or from external sources?

The solar plexus symbolizes the energetic sun, the wellspring from which you extract energy to fuel your ambitions. Whenever you hold an intention, you need to summon all your energy to initiate action. The energy driving this action springs from the solar plexus. It epitomizes your concentrated energy. This chakra also encapsulates the warrior spirit within you. In this context, it represents your capacity for resilience. Through the solar plexus, you energetically combat ailments and ward off negative energies—antagonistic forces within and outside of you. This chakra is where you experience determination and courage, especially when you need to rally your strengths to act decisively.

Personality Traits

Primarily, Achievers are warriors at their core, and as such, this persona is commonly linked with military leaders, fighters, and conquerors. As a result, this personality type is imbued with a formidable strategic intelligence.

What some perceive as the energetic sun within, Achievers identify as the essence of their being. Envision the magnitude of intensity, the presence, and the sense of power and focus they embody upon entering this world. They are akin to a flame. Their presence is palpable when encountered: they emanate an imposing aura, not necessarily of physical enormity, but of an unspoken intent to conquer. They harbor so much energy within them that they often grapple with how to channel it. Directing so much energy can sometimes pose a challenge, leading them to create goals merely as an outlet. They inherently feel an urge to transition from one victory to the next. They harbor no fear of accompanying struggles, for the conception of life as a battlefield resonates with them. The objective here is not to "fight" in the restrictive sense of combating another, but to overcome, including surmounting personal limitations, fears, hesitations, and doubts. They thrive on the experience of transcending obstacles and vanquishing both internal and external foes.

This also influences how Achievers craft the narrative of their life. If this chakra type was asked to recount their life story, it would predominantly circle around victories and failures, trials and setbacks, triumphs and accomplishments. Their instinctive emphasis would be on their upward journey of success, how they've surpassed their own expectations, and the social standing they've achieved. They might share tidbits about failure, but only sparingly, as these are instances they would rather leave behind. If they did delve into challenging times, it would be to highlight the resulting triumph and victory that followed.

For Achievers, life is realized through the lens of ambition; they feel the drive to tap into their potential and aim for illustrious goals. When they pinpoint their target, understand the path forward, acknowledge the impending stretch, and push their limits, that's when they find themselves in a state of bliss. They envision life as an evolutionary journey, but not in the way the root chakra type does, where evolution represents building layer upon layer. Instead, Achievers see life as a process of personal growth, an upward movement, and a saga of self-conquest. Their most ecstatic moments arise when they conquer specific barriers and sense their own power escalating and expanding.

For Achievers, the notion of victory and emerging as a winner represents the epitome of human nobility. Their vision is fixated on the summit, and frankly, they seldom notice anything else. They lift their gaze and proclaim "Behold, there it is!" and "it" always symbolizes the pinnacle of success and power. However, it's crucial to understand that "success" here isn't confined to the narrow definition of being triumphant—even though this aligns perfectly with their preferred reality. It is more about pushing their boundaries, setting audacious goals, and embracing the belief that the sky isn't their ceiling. Thus, their success lies in demonstrating to themselves and others what can be achieved, transforming the seemingly impossible into the possible. It is to this end that they dedicate their days and nights, continually hopping from one peak to another.

Individuals with a primary solar plexus chakra can be identified across all walks of life, from warriors, soldiers, martial artists, executives, politicians, lawyers, entrepreneurs, and coaches to corporate magnates, Olympic athletes, ambitious yogis, monks, rappers, and members of heavy metal bands. Essentially, they are individuals who revel in the sense of power and triumph.

In terms of their distinguishing strengths, these individuals have exceptional self-discipline. They possess a notable sense of self-respect and dignity. Being ardent workers, they constantly strive for excellence. Consequently, they maintain a ceaseless rhythm of productivity and are adept at managing challenging schedules and meeting deadlines. Their energy levels are high, bordering on astounding. They stand out as fiercely independent entities, natural leaders, and innate strategists.

Regarding their potential shortcomings, arguably the most notable limitation for Achievers is their disinterest in engaging with emotion. For them, this perceived insensitivity actually serves as an advantage, as their forward momentum remains unhampered by fluctuating feelings. However, from the perspective of those around them, this emotional disconnection can be seen as a significant flaw, often leading to accusations of coldness. With their sights firmly set on their goals, they may inadvertently treat others as mere stepping stones to their success. They may also demonstrate impatience, a fiery temper, and, at times, anger and rage.

Moreover, individuals dominated by the solar plexus chakra often push themselves to the brink of exhaustion and burnout due to their pursuit of seemingly unattainable goals. During times of overwhelming pressure, they may resort to substance use and harmful habits. Consequently, they may lead lifestyles marked by imbalance, characterized by insufficient rest, unhealthy eating habits, and indulgence in alcohol or cigarettes. An additional shortcoming lies in their perpetual self-comparison, as they often measure their worth against others', asking, "Am I as accomplished as they are?" or "Why are they more successful?" Their relentless desire to win often drives them toward self-serving objectives, centered around wealth, fame, or being the top performer. This is why they could benefit from guidance, but they may only be receptive to it after experiencing severe failure. It is in moments of setback that they may become humble enough to seek assistance.

Solar plexus chakra types harbor an intrinsic fear of failure. The thought of becoming insignificant terrifies them. When they feel unseen, they believe they are virtually nonexistent, as their identity hinges on their actions and achievements. Consequently, Achievers exist in a realm of constant comparison, because it's through this contrast that their existence is validated. If you strip them of their accomplishments and active narratives, what remains? This exact void engulfs them during moments of failure, leaving them perplexed and unable to cope. When failures inevitably occur, they secretly vow to validate their worth, no matter the cost. They nurse thoughts like *One day, I will prove them wrong!* and dedicate their abundant energy toward fulfilling this purpose.

How do individuals who have a primary solar plexus chakra achieve equilibrium? Bear in mind the initial law of balance within the system: it always originates from self-acceptance. For Achievers, this means disregarding voices that caution "Don't overexert," "Cease the relentless quest for accomplishment," and "Take it easy." Their internal flame cannot be extinguished. They were born with it, and thus they should embrace it. However, balance can be found when Achievers realize their inherent worth even when they are in the background. Worthiness is a birthright, irrespective of their position on the scale of victory or defeat. Life, after all, is an amalgamation of failures and successes, and it becomes skewed when only cherishing the ascents. What about life's descents? These periods hold particular implications, values, and teachings too, perhaps even more enlightening ones. Furthermore, Achievers need to shape an identity that endures the highs and lows. They should seek steady equilibrium and a realistic perspective, regardless of life's variations. Their existence should not depend on others validating them or moments of success. Therefore, for an Achiever, transformation lies in acknowledging that profound power resides not in the world, but in independence from it. When they are able to cultivate inner strength independent from external validation, they have found their inner core.

It is strongly advised for individuals with a primary solar plexus chakra to engage in meditation. However, they must be cautious not to transform their meditation into yet another objective or form of achievement. Ideally, meditation should focus on unveiling a facet of life that remains unfazed by peaks and unafraid of valleys.

The Secondary Solar Plexus Chakra Type

When the solar plexus chakra is a secondary chakra type, it infuses the primary chakra with a potent, achievement-focused direction. For example, if an individual's primary chakra is the throat chakra (characterized by inspiration, influence, and shared vision), the solar plexus addition transforms them into a proactive and goal-oriented person—they are no longer purely visionary. The individual's persona is infused with a passion that compels them to actualize their core essence into tangible accomplishments. Consequently, they find fulfillment through the creation of goals, tasks, and strategies. They become focused on leading themselves and others toward success. They derive satisfaction as the leader, the strategist, guiding the way.

Similarly, anyone who has the solar plexus as a secondary chakra type gains a significant ability to realize their ambitions, as this becomes their mode of fulfillment and their primary mechanism for manifestation.

The Supportive Solar Plexus Chakra Type

For those whose supportive chakra is the third chakra, this implies that their source of power and nourishment comes from the solar plexus. Consequently, they have an enduring energy that provides a steady reservoir of vitality regardless of their primary and secondary chakra types. Their most potent source of nourishment and empowerment arises from their ability to actualize their ambitions. While this may be less intense for supportive types than for those who have the solar plexus as their secondary chakra, it functions as a perpetual fuel source, equipping them with exceptional tenacity and resilience. The solar plexus chakra bestows upon them the ability to persist tirelessly, which could be a considerable boon for self-actualization.

Collecting Your Thoughts

Pause for a moment and reflect on whether this depiction resonates with your life experiences. Try to quantify your connection to this description in terms of a general percentage.

The Emotional-Communicative Types
(Caretakers and Speakers)

While the material-earthly types were captivated by the offerings of the physical world, the emotional-communicative types offer a more subtle experience. A subtle experience doesn't necessarily imply a superior or improved one, only that these chakra types gradually lose interest in the material world, favoring instead internal elements such as feelings, visions, concepts, and spiritual states. In this context, as one ascends the ladder of chakras, the object of their fascination becomes increasingly refined.

These chakra types emphasize interpersonal dynamics—the ways people connect, influence each other, and discover a shared or suitable language. Before delving into this group, take a moment to say goodbye to the three lower chakras: the root chakra nestled deep within the perineum, the sacral chakra concealed behind the pubic bone, and the solar plexus chakra located at the center of the body. These chakras form the bedrock of life, akin to the roots and trunk of the existential tree. Standing on this solid ground, leap toward the heart chakra.

The Heart Chakra Type (Caretakers)

The heart chakra is located at the base of the sternum, in the heart of the chest. Attune yourself to this glowing heart center. This chakra grapples with subjects such as relationships, the self and other, the divide between one another, and all the interactions that occur in this space. It also involves the exchange of emotion and explores the universe of emotions at large. Keep in mind that emotions—distinct from feelings—are related to your interactions with others, based on how near or far you perceive yourself to be from them.

This inevitably brings up the desire for unity—the sensation of oneness one may identify as love—contrasting with experiences of detachment, isolation, or loneliness. Other pertinent issues include healing, self-care, emotional self-nurturing, and caring for others. The act of caring introduces concepts of acceptance, learning to encompass another's world, and compassion. However, the heart chakra also poses the challenge of finding the perfect equilibrium between giving and receiving. At its core, the heart chakra prompts expansion from self-centeredness toward sensitivity to others and, eventually, toward universal love. This is the monumental task of evolving your emotional capacity and your ability to love.

Personality Traits

For this chakra type, the world is a stage wholly committed to emotional exchange. The world's purpose is for interacting emotionally and, through this interaction, achieving a true sense of unity and closeness. Propelled by this fervent vision, Caretakers boast a high degree of emotional intelligence, able to profoundly experience emotions and to navigate life guided by these emotional currents.

Given that the essence of life revolves around relationships and interpersonal connections, this chakra type may find themselves preoccupied or troubled, often for the better part of the day, by certain interactions. While other chakra types might also contemplate people and previous conversations, the heart chakra type's focus is due to their constant longing to connect and the contrasting sensation of distance. They harbor a desire to bridge this divide, to understand others and foster mutual comprehension. Consequently, their mental engagement takes a different form.

For Caretakers, emotions are the glue that binds humans together, and this holds true even in interactions such as conducting business. Even in situations involving collaboration and joint ventures, what genuinely matters to the Caretaker is not profit generation, a potential accomplishment, or even their self-expression or self-fulfillment. Their goal is to experience emotional fulfillment and to discover a shared emotional space. And since this is their source of joy, a heart chakra type yearns for peace and harmony above all else. This desire for peace and harmony often supersedes the need to express their views or to be acknowledged as correct. Their yearning might seem somewhat similar to the root chakra type's, since Builders also harbor an intense longing for peace and harmony. However, for Caretakers, this is not simply due to a desire for law and order, but a wish to maintain the integrity of their connections.

Inevitably, this chakra type will experience a potent emotional dependency, particularly on an ultimate other. This point is crucial; for a Caretaker, there must always be an ultimate other (or others)—an individual they can direct a significant portion of their emotional devotion to. Caretakers constantly consider how to meet this individual's needs and bring them happiness. Occasionally, their ultimate other might be someone who passed away but continues to live in their inner world. Thus, Caretakers naturally possess a heightened capacity for care and sensitivity to others' needs, which they feel driven to direct toward particular individuals.

Intense emotions dictate the instances that heart chakra types consider to be their happiest and most significant. Predominantly, these are the moments when Caretakers achieved a sense of unity in relationships, when they succeeded in feeling an unshakable intimacy, or there are moments when they managed to form connections through the heart, like helping a couple who failed to understand each other bond emotionally. These moments are significant for a Caretaker because through intellect alone, empathy and a sense of unity can be hard to find, if not impossible.

Thus, Caretakers aim to witness the victory of the heart: the capability to dismantle barriers and dissolve painful feelings of separation. This applies to people and also to religious experiences, where they commune with God, nature, or the universe. They pursue these moments of profound closeness as their gateway to the meaning of life.

Another deeply meaningful moment for a heart chakra type is when they care for someone and witness their happiness, recovery, or relief from suffering. For many Caretakers, this desire becomes their life's mission, which often manifests in their professional life. Therefore, they are commonly found in fields such as therapy, coaching, and healing, including roles like doctors and nurses. Many Caretakers are also devoted family members who find purpose in ensuring their family's well-being. They also excel as activists, propelled by the desire to protect defenseless beings, including animals or plants.

The Caretaker's fulfillment doesn't come from being an influential public speaker; instead, they find immense satisfaction in direct, one-on-one communication. They typically engage with smaller, intimate groups or just one or two individuals. Caretakers are also found among mediators, peacemakers, and anyone skilled in facilitating understanding between people in conflict or disagreement.

When it comes to their virtues, Caretakers have incredible emotional depths. They are endowed with an impressive capacity for care and healing, and they innately possess therapeutic skills. They also demonstrate a remarkable selflessness, able to put aside their personal concerns when necessary. They have a natural talent for creating intimate connections and heart-to-hearts. As their life revolves around their heart chakra, they exude a natural warmth and gentleness that makes it easy for others to relax around them, contrasting with the relentlessly energetic and ambitious individuals associated with the solar plexus chakra type.

In terms of their potential weaknesses, Caretakers often demonstrate a predisposition toward self-sacrifice and surrender. They dismiss their own voice too quickly. They might say, "It's okay, disregard what I said. Let's do as you suggest," because their primary desire is for peace and connection. They also exhibit a tendency to accept blame too readily, even in situations they are not responsible for. Given their inclination toward self-sacrifice, a Caretaker is particularly susceptible to relinquishing their true self. They often suppress and disregard the values inherent in their own chakra type, and they can find it quite challenging to reestablish their connection to their heart chakra identity.

Consequently, Caretakers may develop intense dependencies and harbor deep-seated, often subconscious fears of loss and abandonment. The terror of abandonment, of losing the love they have managed to foster or discover, can render them overly possessive and excessively attached, leading to a surprising degree of self-concern. While one of their strengths is the ability to deflect focus from themselves, they can also become obsessively self-focused, with the mindset of "This love is mine." As a result, they may deal with issues regarding attachment and possessiveness, and also an extreme sensitivity; Caretakers can be deeply wounded by remarks that are slightly indifferent or lacking in affection.

The primary conflict in the life of a heart chakra type revolves around the dichotomy of dependency and autonomy. This conflict stems from their sense of being one half, constantly seeking their other half. Fundamentally, they perceive themselves as incomplete beings, leading to a profound reliance on the recognition of others to validate their existence. Without such acknowledgment, they feel virtually nonexistent. This echoes the dynamics of those with a primary solar plexus chakra, who similarly feel incomplete if something is subtracted from them, though in the case of Achievers, this is worldly accomplishment and authority. Just as Achievers depend on outside elements for their self-esteem, Caretakers confront this acute dependency as an existential reality.

Under the influence of this deep-seated dependency, Caretakers are persistently plagued by insecurity. This uncertainty is a defining feature of the heart chakra type, manifesting as emotional and existential anxiety. To counterbalance their fear of loss and abandonment, they tend to sacrifice themselves in a disingenuous manner. They start assuming excessive responsibility for others primarily to induce dependency on themselves. The rationale is straightforward: others will feel obligated to them—they may even find it impossible to exist without them! Consequently, Caretakers give more and more to foster this interdependency, though their overzealous self-sacrifice can lead to exhaustion. This behavior masks their deepest fears: abandonment, desertion, and disappointment. Naturally, Caretakers cannot always evade these harrowing situations, yet when emotional setbacks and loss of affection occurs, these moments deeply scar heart chakra types, haunting them throughout their lives as their most profound traumas.

As is invariably the case, the journey toward equilibrium is initiated through self-acceptance. This acceptance entails acknowledging the sheer beauty that lies in the Caretaker's intense focus on others, as well as the allure of their profound yearning for emotional connection. This is not just a gift, but also a talent and a beacon of inspiration for all. Therefore, it is advisable for Caretakers to allow themselves to dwell within the heart, recognizing it as a reservoir of strength. However, this doesn't mean they should completely embody their type without any adjustments. The journey to equilibrium begins with establishing a degree of independence through personal growth, individual therapy, and spiritual teachings and practices, even if their inherent tendency is to lean the other way.

In addition, Caretakers must understand that not everyone is created like them, and that accepting others as they truly are is an essential part of learning to love. Their inability to recognize that others may not share their same sensitivity, lovingness, and emotional depth can easily turn into a sense of superiority or a form of criticism, or disappointed expectations at the very least. Furthermore, their understanding of love is not necessarily comprehensive or fully matured. Caretakers have much to explore when it comes to developing the concept and experience of love. After all, true love transcends codependency or the need for recognition, and what they often perceive as love is, in actuality, a form of insecurity. Love is neither selfish nor possessive, nor does it require an inauthentic self-sacrifice.

The Secondary Heart Chakra Type

For those who have a secondary heart chakra type, fulfillment is achieved through emotional expression. Given that this is their path to self-realization, they will be motivated to seek opportunities to form interpersonal bonds. This quest won't be restricted to personal relationships but will extend to their professional life as well, shaping the way they express themselves in their career. True satisfaction in life will be experienced through a relationship. Consequently, they will always be in pursuit of the ultimate companion, and the majority of their life will assume the structure of a collaborative endeavor. Thus, partnerships and profound connections become the driving force behind fulfillment, fostering creativity and productivity. Typically, their quest for connection will involve the search for an ideal partner who can facilitate fulfillment in the world.

The Supportive Heart Chakra Type

When the heart chakra is an individual's supportive chakra type, it acts as their nurturing and empowering component. This suggests that their source of strength in life is their relationships. The Caretaker's deep-seated emotional bonds and reliable relationships are their wellsprings of energy, particularly during times of depletion. They are pillars of support, a safe harbor. Therefore, whenever they need a surge of motivation to tackle an action or challenge, it is in these relationships that they should seek refuge.

Collecting Your Thoughts

Now, take a moment to reflect upon the percentage to which these traits align with your personal values. Consider how deeply you feel entrenched in the heart chakra as both a personality type and as your soul's imprint. Be sure to record your assessment.

The Throat Chakra Type (Speakers)

Ascend beyond the heart chakra and anchor yourself in the throat chakra, nestled behind the throat's bulge. As you connect with this region, consider the fundamental aspects related to this chakra. At the forefront is self-expression: the ability to vocalize your inner self. This involves unveiling your internal realm—your profound secrets, truths, and identities—and projecting them into the tangible, observable world. The conundrum that resonates with the throat chakra is how to build a bridge between the concealed inner universe—encompassing all your acquired knowledge, insights, and authentic viewpoints—and the outer world. How can we communicate these elements responsibly and transparently in a way that others can comprehend? This naturally brings up the subject of voicing your truth and the matter of justice. Are you articulating your truth in a manner that allows you to stand your ground and make your voice heard? This segues into the equally significant theme of manifestation: the extent to which you can actualize your dreams, visions, and aspirations; connect with your profound potential; and realize it to the fullest. While there's always a need for some level of compromise between one's internal and external realities, there's an essential degree of self-realization required to authentically exist in the world.

Personality Traits

Through the eyes of an individual with a primary throat chakra, the world becomes a platform and opportunity for expression and impact. Their role is to leave a mark, shape the world, and contribute to its evolution. The world also serves as a stage for the actualization of their true self and the realization of their loftiest dreams and visions. Whatever lies within them can be likened to seeds of potential. Every idea, thought, plan, or dream marks the start of a journey toward manifestation. Thus, for those led by the throat chakra, the ultimate value lies in expressing their truth and fulfilling their most profound potential.

Yet individuals of the throat chakra type aren't entirely self-focused, as they also aspire to help others reach similar heights. This desire reflects their approach to influencing others. Driven by the chakra of justice, Speakers pursue fairness. They seek this in forms of societal transformation, social reform, life-altering ideas, and their ability to forge a new world through innovative thoughts and visions. They continually explore the realm of possibilities, hunting for dormant potential that can be ignited.

For Speakers, the focus is primarily on the future. They are characterized by their future-oriented nature, bearing some resemblance to the solar plexus chakra type in this aspect. However, the Speaker's conception of the future is less about concrete goals and more about dreams and visions, much like Martin Luther King Jr.'s "I Have a Dream" speech. It's about the realm of possibility. Hence, what truly propels Speakers is not the exhilaration of conquest but the thrill of manifestation, of bringing grand dreams to life. In this context, throat chakra individuals are the architects and crafters of the future. They show little interest in maintaining or improving the existing reality, unlike root chakra types. Instead, their aspiration is to conceive an entirely new reality. In their minds, there is limitless potential from which they draw inspiration. Consequently, they are always gazing toward the future. Most Speakers have a somewhat dreamy disposition, as they are mentally beyond the present.

Speakers find purpose and joy in successfully influencing others and catalyzing significant change in one's life. A Speaker's elation is at its zenith when they witness someone altering their life trajectory in response to their influence. They take immense pleasure in propagating ideas and concepts they are passionate about, and they aim to make these ideas widespread in the hopes that they will resonate with as many people as possible. As natural leaders—both in their own perception and in practice—Speakers derive satisfaction from inspiring others to follow their lead. They envision themselves as orchestra conductors, harmonizing diverse elements to achieve a synergistic collaboration. With this intention in mind, they cherish the act of uniting individuals and forces, and they possess a remarkable knack for it. Their ambition is to make a meaningful contribution to the world, and they aspire to leave a legacy. Speakers are innately equipped with the skills to shepherd a dream from inception to fruition. However, sometimes there are hindrances in the journey from the dream's genesis to its actualization, which will be discussed in the following pages.

Speakers are predominantly found among those who deliver lectures. Their fondness for verbal communication, especially in-depth discussions, leads them to roles such as educators, coaches, editors, journalists, publicists, and writers (particularly those writers driven by a distinct vision or message). Speakers often emerge as an influencer of sorts. They may be activists, but their form of activism tends to be more revolutionary and centered around justice or the future, unlike the activism of the heart chakra type. Speakers can also be artists who view themselves as conveyors of messages, even when their medium is nonverbal, like music or photography. As artists, they employ their medium to disseminate specific knowledge or ideas. Furthermore, Speakers can be found among politicians, diplomats, and lawyers, especially those who revel in speaking to the court and leading a public life. In essence, they can be identified in any field that facilitates the influence of others and the dissemination of ideas.

Among the distinct strengths associated with the throat chakra is an undeniable charisma and a commanding presence. There's an inherent charm that makes them naturally attractive. They are gifted communicators and writers. However, their inclination for expression doesn't always imply a desire to address crowds. Many Speakers prefer to disseminate ideas through writing or other less-direct methods. These individuals possess a remarkable ability to adapt their communication based on the audience's needs, understanding their perspectives and identifying what they require at any given moment.

Moreover, throat chakra types have a unique ability to recognize and appreciate transformative ideas, including groundbreaking technological innovations that promise a brighter future for humanity and alleviate suffering. They can deftly translate complex ideas into easily understood concepts. Beyond just simplifying these notions, Speakers demonstrate how these ideas are beneficial and make them easily relatable.

Another notable characteristic of throat chakra types is their capacity to weave together ideas from various fields, synthesizing them into one coherent message. Speakers serve as bridges, facilitating the flow of information from different worlds and allowing these worlds to enrich each other. This knack for creating connections makes them proficient at forming networks of people and teams, as they recognize common goals that can unite all parties. Lastly, their heightened sensitivity to justice can sometimes transform them into formidable warriors.

However, along with their strengths, Speakers also bring weaknesses to the table. At times, they display opportunistic tendencies, reshaping themselves to align with whatever the environment demands of them. This adaptive, chameleonlike nature can leave others questioning their true identity, as their personality appears elusive and unclear.

Speakers are also capable of manipulative behavior and may resort to dishonesty to gain influence. They may show a lack of tact and sensitivity toward others' emotions, especially when engrossed in the pursuit of their vision. An innate need for control is also characteristic of throat chakra types, which can sometimes morph into a form of self-righteousness.

Their focus on the distant horizon can make Speakers overly dreamy and unrealistic, leading to impatience with slow, meticulous processes that require careful attention to detail. They may struggle to comprehend why a vision—which, in their mind, has already manifested—still needs to be actualized. Speakers often wonder, *If I can visualize it so clearly, why isn't it already there?* This perspective can breed laziness, as they prefer directing others over engaging in hard work themselves. They relish their role as commanders, and when faced with demanding tasks, their patience can quickly dwindle.

Speakers often grapple with a core tension in their lives: the drive to actualize their dreams and visions against the stubborn and unyielding nature of reality. They find themselves perpetually caught in the crossfire between their dreams and their reality. This chasm between what is and what could be brings them great distress, amplified by their acute awareness of the possible.

Consequently, a divide emerges between their perception and concrete reality, leading to resistance and a reluctance to fully immerse themselves in the real world. Unwilling to compromise, they embody a "my way or the highway" attitude. Speakers not only strive to superimpose their vision onto reality, they also tell others how to think and behave. In their minds, they have a meticulously crafted script, and they expect others to follow it, even when they haven't been explicitly informed of their roles. When things don't transpire as the Speaker imagined, their discontent is palpable. The feelings of others may be sidelined, as the throat chakra type is primarily driven by the pursuit of their *own* dreams and visions. When the disparity becomes seemingly insurmountable, Speakers often retreat, either inwardly or outwardly proclaiming, "If that's the case, I'm out!" They may abandon their projects or, more broadly, withdraw from life. They cease all activity and refuse to press on, sticking steadfastly to their plan. This obstinacy can lead to significant trauma when they collide head-on with the harsh realities of life.

In their journey toward equilibrium, Speakers need to embrace their inherent nature. It's perfectly acceptable for them to dream big, to keep their head in the clouds, and to be naturally predisposed toward the future and ambitious—even seemingly outlandish—aspirations. This is their authentic self, and it is something they should relish.

However, this inclination needs to be tempered with an understanding that dreams only become reality when the world consents. Speakers need to adopt a humbler approach to reality and people. They must recognize that they're not puppeteers in a grand puppet show. This leads to an unfamiliar term in the vocabulary of the throat chakra type: *flexibility*. Speakers need to learn to allow reality to mold their dreams and visions, to be open to the possibility of even better outcomes, and to practice listening rather than being preoccupied with making themselves heard.

The Secondary Throat Chakra Type

If the throat chakra is an individual's secondary chakra type, they essentially take on the role of a teacher or educator. Regardless of what their primary chakra type might be, they derive fulfillment from teaching and sharing ideas. Typically, the ideas they spread are tied to the fundamental values of their primary chakra type. Ultimate fulfillment lies in expressing these ideas and making an impact on the world. This unique alignment endows the Speaker with a robust capacity for self-expression via writing, teaching, speaking, and educating. They hold immense influence over others through their ideas. Nothing within them can stay concealed; everything must immediately find form and be expressed, thereby shaping the world around them. So, if the throat chakra emerges as one's secondary type, they are gifted with an extraordinary ability to manifest the essence of their primary chakra type.

The Supportive Throat Chakra Type

If the throat chakra is one's supportive chakra type, their empowerment and nourishment derive from self-expression, self-fulfillment, and influencing others. This doesn't consume them as it might if the throat chakra was their primary or secondary type. Rather, it serves as a substantial motivational force that is often a stabilizing factor for softer or less-grounded chakras. This lends an intriguing facet to the individual's blueprint, fueling a quest for influence, the pursuit of their voice, and a search for their truth.

Collecting Your Thoughts

Take a moment to tune in to your inner self. Gauge how prominent this type is in your value system, in your passions, and in your interpretation of life's purpose. Assess this as a percentage.

The Mental-Spiritual Types (Thinkers and Yogis)

The final two chakras constitute a distinct subgroup often referred to as the *mental-spiritual category*. This cluster addresses abstract concepts, ideas, and intricate relations with both reality and the cosmos. While the throat chakra type was engaged with ideas, this group pursues something even more nuanced and refined.

The Third Eye Chakra Type (Thinkers)

Tune in to the third eye chakra, located deep within the brain, just above the space between the eyebrows. Traditionally dubbed the *guru chakra*, this energy center operates as the wisdom eye, offering a lucid vision and profound understanding of truth that transcends all thoughts, emotions, and opposing inner voices. Thus, when it's unbalanced, the third eye chakra breeds confusion and inner contradiction. This chakra is a sanctuary in the quest for truth and the longing for profound understanding. It's also associated with clear vision and the ability to discern subtler, often invisible, realities. The third eye chakra encapsulates awareness and awakened perception, incorporating detached, objective, and uninvolved observation.

Personality Traits

Those with a primary third eye chakra have an innate penchant for intellect and philosophy. Indeed, their life is primarily the life of the mind. For them, the mind isn't a container for random thoughts; instead, it's an expansive, boundless space. Therefore, the mind becomes an adventurous journey, a source of never-ending exploration.

Thinkers view the world through the lens of the third eye, and from their perspective, life is a landscape for understanding and discovering truth. Their belief is that life's purpose (and the reason they possess a mind) is to understand. Hence, they are explorers on a quest for knowledge and wisdom, just as Artists are adventurers in pursuit of intense feelings and peak experiences.

Thinkers are characterized by a philosophical, curious, and intellectually questioning demeanor. They continually carry the question of "Why?" They delve into the depths that they are convinced lie beneath everything they scrutinize. Their inquisitive and questioning minds lead to a strong tendency to observe things from the periphery and a drive to achieve an objective viewpoint.

Such tendencies, usually evident since early childhood, give Thinkers a scientific disposition. They act as the world's investigators, striving to penetrate the core of things, perpetually looking beneath the surface. For them, everything is a façade, an illusion that needs to be removed in order to uncover the underlying reality. Their ultimate aim is to unravel the enigma of life as a whole, to reach a kind of supreme understanding through the use of their principal tools: concepts. After all, for them, life is understood through abstract ideas or concepts.

Thinkers find a profound sense of purpose and joy when they successfully decipher complex puzzles and challenges. Life attains depth when they pursue, and occasionally formulate, expansive and integrated theories or models. This depth is further enhanced when they partake in intense philosophical debates or spiritual inquiries. Such dialogues are their conduit to experiencing a shared connection with others.

One of the ultimate sources of exhilaration for a Thinker is observing with a quiet and unresponsive mind when a breakthrough dawns upon them. This is the pivotal moment they yearn for—a sort of enlightenment when they witness something with pure, unclouded clarity. Additionally, they derive a sense of meaning when they assimilate new information, discovering something previously unknown to them.

It's not difficult to discern that Thinkers, armed with their acute and luminous intellect, gravitate toward roles such as scholars, researchers, and philosophers. Their aptitude for wielding language with precision and finesse also makes them capable authors. Their ranks include contemplative monks and passionate pursuers of truth. The Thinker's innate capacity to probe the depths of the human psyche can lead to a fulfilling career in psychology. More broadly, they can be found among those with an insatiable appetite for learning—individuals who constantly seek out educational opportunities, from short courses to master's degrees, purely for the sheer joy and gratification derived from learning.

The Thinker's capabilities are inherently tied to the vibrancy of their sixth chakra. Consequently, they often exhibit a radiant intelligence characterized by lucid understanding and bright insight. These individuals delve deep, never settling for incomplete or subpar answers. Their intellectual prowess is evident in their capacity to think differently, push boundaries, and unearth solutions. In addition, they excel at formulating models and theories. Thinkers are typically gifted with quick minds, enabling them to effortlessly grasp complex ideas and swiftly discern the interconnectivity of things. Fueled by their desire to facilitate ongoing introspection and influenced by their honorable nature, they lead lives marked by structure and dignity, fostering a sense of mastery over their existence. Their profound independence and natural detachment define their free-spirited essence.

These third eye inclinations give rise to certain character flaws. Thinkers are prone to seclusion, as their intense focus can lead them to overlook communicating with others. Their deep absorption in their studies or internal reflections often result in self-imposed isolation. Engaging with life and experiencing it without the constant interference of their analytical thoughts, which tirelessly aim to "understand," can be a challenge. Even in situations where others might immerse themselves in the moment, Thinkers keep a vigilant and observing mind, insisting on comprehension. They frequently retreat into their minds, maintaining an aloof perspective, which often results in the evasion of real-life experiences. Their personalities are punctuated by intense criticism and suspicion, and they always seek ulterior motives behind others' actions, leading to constant questioning of intent. Furthermore, Thinkers can exhibit extreme arrogance, potentially making them the most self-important among all chakra types. From their intellectual high ground, they often dismiss those they deem less intelligent. Lastly, much like the root chakra type, they often become excessively tied to routines and schedules, insisting on punctuality and meticulous planning to avoid mundane distractions.

The fundamental narrative of the third eye chakra type revolves around their desire to comprehend life through observation and study, nearly bypassing the realm of firsthand experience. Their mantra is "If I've grasped something mentally, why do I need the actual experience? I understand it!" This mentality distances them from life, as their overconfidence convinces them that they have sufficiently grasped life via their intellectual constructs. Consequently, they feel an intense sense of disconnection from the collective. It's as if they perceive themselves to be outsiders, alien to the human experience. However, they harbor a secret desire—a desire they seldom acknowledge due to their intense pride—to become integrated with the world and those in it. Thus, they find themselves caught in a tug-of-war between these opposing forces. Traumatic memories typically revolve around this tension between inclusion and exclusion. Thinkers aim to navigate this lifetime untouched, aspiring to keep their hands clean of the messiness of life without acknowledging that they've journeyed through it. Therefore, Thinkers are conflicted—they don't want to engage, yet they lack the know-how to truly belong, which only feeds their growing arrogance.

Individuals of the third eye chakra type can find balance by embracing the fact that they will, in some way, perpetually feel disconnected and uninvolved. An inherent aloofness will persist within them, despite their best efforts. This is because they tend to inhabit their observing mind, where life's intensity is most profoundly experienced. However, they should work to remove the self-defense elements that often create an exaggerated distance. This defense was created out of a need for self-protection, a desire to feel unique, and a fear of direct experience. Another crucial understanding lies in recognizing that life cannot be fully comprehended through abstract concepts alone, as a significant portion of life is understood solely through experience. A Thinker cannot philosophize their way through life, nor can they completely rationalize life's essence.

The Secondary Third Eye Chakra Type

If the third eye chakra is an individual's secondary chakra type, this means that regardless of their primary type, they utilize the mind as a platform for learning, research, and discovery. Ultimately, their purpose and fulfillment lie in the acquisition of wisdom, no matter what their primary chakra type is. In other words, they manifest their primary chakra type through the constant pursuit of knowledge and idea generation, akin to an eternal learner. This journey will lead to a life of investigation and scholarship, even if their main motivation springs from elsewhere. For instance, if their primary chakra type is the heart chakra, they will be propelled to study the topics or individuals they love in order to attain wisdom.

The Supportive Third Eye Chakra Type

In a supportive role, the third eye chakra acts as a recharging and empowering influence. These Thinkers derive the most satisfaction when they engage the philosophical and intellectual facets of their existence. Nurturing a lifelong commitment to knowledge is the conduit for their energy. As such, they will always feel the need to learn something, to stay connected to processes of intellectual growth. While it might not be their primary influence, the third eye chakra serves as an immense source of sustenance, offering inspiration and catalyzing their development in alignment with their primary and secondary chakra types.

Collecting Your Thoughts

Take a moment to assess and quantify the presence of the third eye chakra type within you. Express it as a percentage.

The Crown Chakra Type (Yogis)

Ascend to the pinnacle of the chakra system to find the crown chakra, nestled deep within the brain, beneath the crown of the head. This chakra doesn't primarily serve a psychological function. Rather, it governs awareness of connection to the supreme self, infinity, and divinity. It also oversees the dissolution of egoic boundaries and the experience of transcendence. This encompasses a quest for the eternal and absolute truth, as well as the willingness to sever ourselves from earthly ties and achieve nonattachment and spiritual liberation. The crown chakra also determines your ability to immerse yourself in profound silence and explore the depths of meditation.

Personality Traits

Those with a dominant crown chakra possess extraordinary spiritual wisdom. Aspects that others might study for years—such as mastering silence, meditation, and the comprehension of spiritual tenets—come naturally to them. The majority of their attention is not invested in the physical universe. Their interest in the tangible world is rather limited compared to their fascination with the spiritual aspect of life—the fountainhead of existence, the unchanging truths. They perceive life not as a physical journey but as a pathway to liberation, a chance to free themselves from earthly attachments, and they consider life to be a sequence of spiritual challenges. To them, life is a succession of spiritual tests, each serving as a stepping stone toward ultimate freedom.

The crown chakra type, known as the Yogi, emanates an almost ethereal personality, teetering on the brink of nonexistence. This quality is often perceptible even in their physical form, which appears somewhat translucent. They lack a strong attachment or sense of possessiveness. Material possessions, accumulation of wealth, and the obtaining of physical objects scarcely interest them. Their disinterest in worldly human values is stark. They are irresistibly drawn to the unseen, the astral and transcendent dimensions, the realms one could refer to as celestial. They may establish deep connections with spiritual entities and find themselves captivated by the magical, including interactions with unseen forces and experiences beyond the confines of the physical body. They are intrigued by concepts such as the dissolution of self and deep self-absorption. A strong desire to lead a life of purity, both internally and externally, propels them. Hence, it could be said that their primary focus lies in existing rather than merely living: their purpose is to learn and master the art of being.

Addressing the Yogi's perception of life's meaning can be tricky, since they don't find earthly existence inherently significant, except as an avenue for spiritual liberation or ascension. They find the utmost joy in immersing themselves in seclusion, surrendering entirely to their spiritual pursuits. Bliss involves basking in silence, when they can shrug off the weight of earthly gravity to ascend into the spiritual cosmos, and when they can chase their passion without any constraints. They experience joy during profound and spiritually resonant moments, especially when they sense an intimate closeness with the divine. They also take great pleasure in being part of a community devoted to spiritual pursuits. Thus, you may encounter them among yogis, hermits, spiritual guides, meditation instructors, monks, shamans, and even practitioners of the arcane arts.

Yogis possess several unique strengths and virtues. They are notably gentle and benign beings, equipped with a robust capacity for lengthy, intensive meditation. Their grasp of spiritual matters is swift and intuitive. They display a notable lack of attachment to worldly possessions and exhibit a sense of lightness, almost as if they're floating on air. They are characteristically unselfish, demonstrating a distinct lack of preoccupation with their personal fate.

Certain drawbacks can be discerned in those with a crown chakra personality, such as an imbalanced urge to dissolve, vanish, and disconnect entirely from the world. This excessive yearning can lead them down various paths. For instance, they may display a reckless lifestyle, steering clear of responsibilities and sidestepping life's challenges. Their lack of worldly ambition often translates into disinterest in accomplishing anything. Their apathy toward money is so extreme that it impairs their ability to maintain their own livelihood. They may also consider themselves excessively sensitive and feel too gentle, frail, or delicate to cope with life's merciless aspects.

These inclinations mold the primary narrative of Yogis, the core struggle they grapple with in life: the sentiment that their true abode is not on earth and cannot be located here, because they belong to the spiritual realm. They yearn to return home, or to retreat into seclusion and bide their time until they can make their way home. They are engulfed in fundamental confusion:

"Why am I here? What is my purpose here?" They resist existing in this world and dealing with life's hurdles and daily obligations; their sole desire is to shed this weight so that it can be taken up by someone else. Indeed, they often end up entrusting others with these responsibilities. This leads them to develop a reliance on others, including financially. So, they are caught in the tension between physical existence and what they perceive as their only home.

Just like every other chakra type, the path to balance begins with acceptance. Yogis must first embrace their unique and rare nature, a task that is not easy when the majority of the world doesn't uphold their values. This can lead to an identity crisis, with many crown chakra individuals unaware of their type due to their suppressed nature and an inability to grasp their unique traits—they often navigate life in a state of confusion, particularly within the existing world dynamics.

Nonetheless, it's crucial for Yogis to find some form of balance, a middle ground of sorts. This is because they need to comprehend that their existence is also an expression of divine intent. People were not aimlessly placed here—existence is not a mistake or a mere coincidence. The divine has not erred, and none of us are lost wanderers in the world. Existence holds a purpose, and it is not solely to remain an unlimited entity immersed in a state of pure light. If that were the case, humans would have stayed in a condition of void and pure illumination. Hence, there is a need to appreciate that spirituality has a broader definition than merely reverting back to an individual's spiritual essence.

In fact, a key aspect of spiritual life includes learning responsibility—financial responsibility included—and experiencing commitment to other sentient beings or specific values and objectives. Therefore, spirituality involves leading a responsible life. Additionally, Yogis must ensure that their spiritual focus doesn't morph into an elaborate form of self-focus. As they become increasingly self-absorbed, they risk becoming indifferent to the needs and desires of others.

The Secondary Crown Chakra Type

When the crown chakra serves as a secondary chakra in one's blueprint, it often results in a fundamental lack of grounding. If an individual has a secondary crown chakra (signifying that their fulfillment is linked to the crown chakra), this pulls their entire essence toward spiritual expression, devotion, and existence. Their primary chakra's features are absorbed by these spiritual energies, compelling them to lead a profoundly spiritual life, a life akin to that of a spiritual mentor or someone whose satisfaction can only be found through a mystical lifestyle. Naturally, this calls for some adaptations. If they continue to reside in Western, modern society, it will be necessary for them to establish their personal version of an ashram within their lifestyle.

The Supportive Crown Chakra Type

If an individual has the crown chakra as their supportive chakra type, it signifies that this is the force that enriches and sustains them throughout their life. Therefore, their utmost source of nourishment is derived from retreats, meditations, connections with spiritual mentors, and indulgence in spiritual studies; every time they find themselves exhausted, this is the primary source of inspiration they should seek. It is crucial to persistently engage in these practices, or else they risk losing their energy source. Spiritual energy should also permeate into who they are (denoted by their primary chakra type) and their life's purpose (represented by their secondary chakra type).

Collecting Your Thoughts

Pause for a while and reflect on the presence of the crown chakra type within you. Assess it in the form of a percentage.

THREE

THE ROAD TO SELF-RECOGNITION

Drawing on the Chakra Flowering technique outlined in chapter 1, conjure up an image of the central channel entwined by all seven energy cores. Adjust your visualization so the three most prominent chakras that you've discerned within your system thus far shine brightly, like lanterns. Experience the radiant trail formed by this triad, its glow emanating from within the central channel. To the best of your understanding at this point, this triad represents your most powerful forces, your most potent energies.

How can you confirm that these are indeed your three most potent chakras and verify their exact configuration? To accurately self-identify your chakra blueprint, I recommend three principal techniques:

1. **The Questionnaire:** In general, this tool provides sufficient clarity about one's primary chakra type. The questionnaire was provided in chapter 2.

2. **The Percentage Evaluation Method:** As you read the detailed profiles of each type in chapter 2, I asked you to simultaneously rank and evaluate the prominence of each type. This approach can be illuminating,

especially when percentages such as 80 percent, 70 percent, or even 10 percent begin to emerge, resulting in a clearer overall picture.

3. **Writing Practices:** The trio of exercises offered in chapter 4 will connect your foundational life experiences and basic constitution.

At this point, you have completed the questionnaire and assessed the prevalence of the seven chakra types within your own blueprint, and you've reached a certain level of self-identification. Ideally, you've identified your primary chakra type. In most cases, the questionnaire and self-assessment are sufficient to attain this inner clarity. You may also have a good sense of your secondary type. Perhaps your chakra blueprint is so glaringly obvious that you've pinpointed your supportive type as well! Yet, if you find yourself wavering at this juncture, rest assured that is totally normal. The aim of chapters 3 and 4 is to alleviate such uncertainties.

For some, self-recognition is a breeze. You may have read one of the descriptions of the seven primary types and instantly knew it was a perfect match. Perhaps you felt an immediate connection and exclaimed, "That's me!" Furthermore, the type you resonated with may have seamlessly corresponded with your questionnaire results. If that's your situation, then your quest ends here. Your task from this point forward is to understand how to apply this newfound self-awareness. You can skip ahead to chapter 4 to learn how to apply what you've discovered.

For the majority of people, a perfect 100 percent match is unlikely. Compatibility with a chakra type will most likely range anywhere between 70 percent to 100 percent. Regardless of the percentage, bear in mind that you are in pursuit of the description that most aligns with your unique self. This depiction should reflect your personal viewpoint, your individual method of perceiving the world, and how you understand and respond to things, as well as what grabs your attention and what fades into the background.

From this perspective, there exist seven distinct paths to happiness and purpose, not just one. There are no universal definitions of happiness or the meaning of life that fit all chakra types. Hence, for some, it's a 100 percent match, case closed. For others, there's a markedly high alignment that clearly sets them apart from the rest. Yet, for some, there may be an internal struggle (multiple chakras vying for supremacy), which is quite normal and, ultimately, profoundly meaningful. So, there's no need to fret or rush the process. Allow the journey of gently merging into your primary chakra type to occur. It will unfold in its own time.

This process may necessitate digging beneath layers of ingrained conditioning and self-suppression. You may have reached such a degree of self-suppression that you've become accustomed to identifying societal norms or familial values as your own. You might also be dealing with a restrictive self-image that prevents clarity; you may have an idea of who you wish to be that obstructs your ability to know yourself with certainty. (Remember, chakra types aren't necessarily about who you aspire to be—they reveal who you authentically *are*.) As such, this journey often requires patience. Don't stress about it; instead, let things take their natural course and observe the outcome once you've finished reading and practicing the exercises in part I, perhaps even part II.

If you are struggling to determine your chakra blueprint, pause and ask yourself if you are plagued by a fear of decision-making. This fear can arise when trying to ascertain your chakra types. Even when you have your answer, you may be too apprehensive and filled with doubt to assert, "All right, this is it!" This fear of arriving at a clear decision actually echoes another underlying pattern. Strive to undergo this process without being afraid of making an error. Most likely, you're already closer to the truth than you think. I'm fairly certain that the percentages you assigned in the previous chapter somewhat reflect your constitution. Maybe not in the exact order, but they're generally accurate. So, be confident that you're already moving in the right direction.

Regardless of your situation, this is a crucial process of self-discovery, of getting to know yourself better. After all, if you can't identify the specific experiences that shape your understanding of life's purpose, can you truly claim to know yourself? If you are unaware of what brings you joy and true fulfillment, this process provides an excellent opportunity to seek those answers.

Determining Your Primary Type, Once and for All

Your primary chakra type serves as the sun around which your secondary and supportive chakras orbit like planets. If you have not yet discerned your primary type, this is a task that can be accomplished through a couple of readily available methods.

Recognizing your primary type doesn't mean you have to align with every minor characteristic mentioned, such as a sacral chakra type's possible aversion to early mornings. These minor aspects can vary, so don't be troubled if things don't perfectly correspond. It's important to remember that these details might shift due to the intricate nature of your chakra blueprint. After all, there are two other influential chakras within your system that maintain balance and influence your disposition in various ways.

Focus your introspection on two questions. First, ask yourself, *What do I truly love?* As you reflect on this question, it will bridge the distance between you and your heart, and your heart, in turn, will bring you closer to your soul. For example, if you answered, *I love watching and listening to people to understand human behavior*, this suggests you might relate to the third eye chakra type. If you answered, *I love helping people heal and easing their pain*, this might mean you resonate with the heart chakra type. Thus, this process is inherently transformative. Through this introspection, you will begin to experience and affirm your unique value system, individual purpose, and life's meaning. This isn't something prescribed or dictated by others. It's a process of connecting with your core essence, your life's passion. Hence, this question initiates a journey that will ultimately bring you closer to your true self, irrespective of societal expectations, self-perception, and preconceived notions of your life's path.

The second question you need to ask yourself is: *What has been my biggest issue with life for as long as I can remember?* This understanding will help you crystallize the key struggle or inherent friction you experience in life. This realization also signifies growing self-awareness, as many people are so engrossed in various conflicts that they fail to identify the underlying tension in their disputes. As you engage with this primary tension, you will start to understand that it is somewhat intrinsic. Recognizing this likely brings relief. This common tension is not merely a negative aspect of life, but more of a lifelong guide—it's there to facilitate your growth. The way you respond to this primal narrative serves as a driving force for your personal evolution.

In the same vein, you'll come to understand that your life's theme isn't personal. You may consider certain struggles to be distinctly yours. However, you'll recognize that your challenges are part of a broader chakra constitution, a more primordial characteristic. For instance, if a Caretaker was to engage in a conversation about their life's theme with another heart chakra type, their themes would essentially align to the same core struggle, despite subtle differences. These challenges exist because the desires of the chakra are often ignored or blocked by life and other people. This realization can be both revealing and liberating. Certain challenges are part of your pattern, not a mistake. They aren't something to eradicate or remove; rather, they are something that you need to engage with—or better yet, dance with.

Of the two questions provided, it may be easier to discern your primary chakra type by confronting your underlying conflict rather than what you love. Why is this? Frequently, people find themselves estranged from the deep-seated desires of their hearts. These passions have slipped from their grasp, and they no longer connect with them on a daily basis. For instance, you might be entrenched in a particular work environment that does not facilitate the manifestation of your primary chakra type. Consequently, you will have molded yourself to meet expectations, tolerating unhappiness or dissatisfaction because it's familiar. As a result, your authentic passion will drift away until you barely recognize yourself. In such a quandary, reconnecting with the fundamental story or inherent stress of your primary chakra type often proves more direct and attainable.

The Next Step: Discerning Your Secondary Chakra Type

The ability to ease into your primary chakra is central to the entire chakra types system. However, it's important to note that remaining true to the values of your primary chakra type merely sets the foundation.

Consider this model that encapsulates the design of your soul. Naturally, the soul forms the core. It's important to note that the soul isn't a specific chakra type; instead, you can think of chakra types as concentric circles rippling out from the soul's core with varying strengths. First, there's the layer of your current personality, embodied by your primary chakra type. It envelops the soul like a protective sheath. Next, there's a layer that shields the core and the innermost layer; this represents your secondary chakra type. Lastly, there's a defensive layer or outermost layer that supports this system, represented by the supportive chakra type. This is a comprehensive perspective of your personality; observe how these layers emanate from the soul like ripples in a pond.

If we only had one layer—the innermost layer, represented by the primary chakra type—we would be mere archetypes. Naturally, this wouldn't be feasible; it's impossible to be solely a root chakra type or strictly a sacral chakra type. That would render people extremely one-dimensional, suggesting only seven personality types in all of existence. Instead, each of us has two more chakra types that start to animate our system, transforming us into vibrant, multifaceted beings. Other influences are needed to foster individuality, and the secondary and supportive chakra types allow us to mature into someone distinct, complete with tendencies, subtleties, and even peculiarities. This structure gives rise to genuine individuality.

However, the question of distinguishing between the primary and secondary chakra types inevitably resurfaces, particularly when two chakra types received a similar percentage. Perhaps one chakra type scored 80 percent and another 85 percent, leading to uncertainty. Despite possible competition amongst chakras, the structure of your chakra blueprint carries significant meaning. The primary chakra reflects your essence—the core of who you are—whereas the secondary chakra is the way in which this essence seeks completion. In this light, your secondary chakra type serves as your medium for manifestation. It's the pathway by which you present yourself to the world, the lifestyle you adopt, and the method you employ to express your inner essence. Consequently, the secondary chakra type operates as a facilitator. Occasionally, its intensity may come close to that of your primary type, and this underscores the critical connection between essence and manifestation. After all, it's the strength of the secondary chakra type that propels you toward fulfillment and actualization.

Think of the first two chakra types as partners in a relationship: one partner is accountable for the interpretation of the world, determining values, significance, and joy, while the other, more pragmatic partner ensures that these principles are actualized in the world. The two function as a singular entity, ideally cooperating in harmony. Generally, the secondary type can have an enhancing or a calming effect on the primary type, which is often quite beneficial. For instance, if you identify as a sacral chakra type, an Artist, wholly immersed in the delight of the present moment, and your secondary chakra type is the solar plexus, the Achiever, it immediately transforms your overall direction toward empowerment. Conversely, if your primary type is the Achiever and your secondary is the Artist, this tempers your intense passion and stimulates a deeper interest in expressing yourself through joy.

What if, within this pairing, both chakra types either temper or amplify each other, leading to an intense inner alignment? You might be an Achiever and a Speaker, forming a rather heated tandem, or a Caretaker and a Yogi, a mix that would render you extremely ethereal and unanchored. In these situations, it becomes essential to navigate these excesses and disparities. But bear in mind, the universe doesn't make mistakes, so there's no need to worry!

In an ideal scenario, the primary and secondary chakra types cooperate and collaborate to foster a harmonious union. However, in reality—and this is where the learning journey takes a truly fascinating turn—the two may at times operate in opposition to one another, resulting in a conflict. This happens when an individual is caught in a state of unawareness, leading to the friction of a misaligned pairing, with two voices tugging in their own directions. Essentially, it's an interpersonal conflict. Consequently, the task becomes learning how to cultivate harmony in this union. This is simply a matter of fostering greater awareness.

Consider, for example, a pairing of the third eye chakra as the primary type and the throat chakra as the secondary. The third eye type, the Thinker, tends to lean toward solitude, showing interest in books and eschewing any influence over others due to their absorption in self-exploration and intellectual pursuits. This type cherishes individuality and enjoys immersing themselves in laboratories, libraries, and home environments without considering how this appears to others. In this example, the individual's secondary chakra type is the throat chakra, the Speaker. Here comes the counterpart, advocating, "Let's share all of this with the world. You need to do this and that. You need to be really intense and perhaps post on Instagram to express yourself." Now, the third eye chakra resists this, does it not? The Thinker prefers to engage with the elevated and refined world, but the Speaker urges toward manifestation, which the Thinker considers superficial and undignified. This is where the friction starts, and the individual's task becomes learning how to transform this into a harmonious flow that originates from the core, moves through the channel of the throat chakra, and balances the system. This is the charm of the chakra types.

By now, you might have begun to explore your own unique combination. That's great! Remember, the secondary type closely aligns with your value system and what matters to you, but it remains slightly distant. It isn't exactly your essence. It's not entirely your authentic self, and it will never truly feel like it is. Try fully immersing yourself in your secondary chakra in order to truly comprehend this.

Let's revisit the example of the third eye chakra type as an individual's primary personality. If someone asserted, "You're entirely a fifth chakra type. You've misunderstood. Now, embrace your true nature as an absolute Speaker," this would be rather uncomfortable, because the third eye chakra type could never truly feel at ease embodying the throat chakra type. That's because, in this combination, the throat chakra only serves as the instrument for manifestation.

This suggests that a crucial hint in determining your primary chakra type is the sensation of being at home. When you're in your own abode, you experience comfort, free from any strain. It's your familiar environment. This is the way your primary chakra type is supposed to feel—even if at times your definition of home might be akin to a house aflame, burning with fervor, similar to the intensity of a solar plexus chakra type, an Achiever.

Your secondary chakra type can be unearthed by posing these questions: *What form does my self-fulfillment take in the world? How do I actualize my true self? How do I express myself?* Your means of expression don't define your identity. Instead, it's the pathway through which you manifest your true self. Consequently, the secondary chakra type is intimately tied to career choices and overall lifestyle. Reflect upon these questions as well: *Is my route to fulfillment teaching others and sharing ideas? Is it through building and nurturing relationships? Or perhaps designing and creating harmonious, efficient systems? Is my form of expression found in the roles of a student, a researcher, a solitary yogi, or an ambitious world conqueror? Is it a lifestyle that exudes joy, brimming with happiness, playfulness, and adventure, wandering from one location to the next?* This introspective process will ensure that you connect with the fundamental essence of your secondary chakra type.

The Final Step: Tapping Into Your
Supportive Chakra Type

You are now at the third and final step—bringing to light your tertiary personality type. This supportive chakra type generally fluctuates between 30 percent and 60 percent, but it could be higher. For example, if your primary type stands at 100 percent, your secondary at 80 percent, and your supportive at 70 percent, this alignment is entirely appropriate. However, if it's less than 30 percent, the chakra might not be a major influence in your life. A 30 percent presence indicates the chakra is quite active in your system. When a chakra reaches 50 percent or 60 percent, it becomes a key part of your personality. Remember, it's not the exact percentages but the intensity of these levels that truly shapes who you are.

Your supportive chakra type doesn't correlate directly with the values of your soul. As you may have grasped from the discussion on the seven primary types in the previous chapter, this chakra acts as your key source of nourishment and empowerment. It is the foundation from which you draw your energy; it's what sustains your momentum and imparts strength to you.

While the supportive chakra type may seem less significant on its own, within the triad of chakra types, it assumes immense importance. It's crucial to acknowledge its role. Once you identify this third chakra type, it completes your holistic understanding of the harmonies and imbalances, the strengths and challenges within your personality. This knowledge empowers you to harmonize these three elements effectively.

Therefore, the probing questions that guide you toward your supportive type are: *What fuels my growth and empowerment? What is the wellspring of my strength that propels me along my life's journey? Is it the solidity of my foundations that bestows this strength? Could it be the delight and happiness I experience? Might it be my aspiration and determination? Is it the emotions and connections in my relationships? Could it be my desire to voice my truths? Is it my passion for learning and my quest for understanding? Or is it possibly linked to meditation and spiritual aspects?*

Undoubtedly, meditation offers inherent nourishment, and maintaining a serene atmosphere at home nurtures all of us. Cultivating harmonious relationships with family members is also a source of nourishment. While all of these aspects can contribute to well-being, your focus here should be on the core energy that imbues you with power and resilience.

This doesn't imply the absence of other potent chakras within your system. It's crucial to understand this, as you may have observed that you possess other chakra types that stand at 30 percent or even 40 percent. This signifies the presence of other strong chakras, which is a positive. You are fortunate, as the more strong connections you have, the more well-rounded you are. Having more than three potent chakras is certainly advantageous. Nevertheless, the three most potent ones will orchestrate the interplay of energies within your personality. This trio of chakras propels your personality forward by prompting you to make decisions, to manifest in particular manners, and to act. These are also the three chakras you need to understand if you want to truly explore self-fulfillment.

In part II, I will provide you with advanced tools to solidify your secondary and supportive chakra types. These tools may help you find clarity or validate the chakra types you have selected. I will also briefly describe the forty-two possible primary and secondary combinations, which will help you better understand how the chakra types coalesce to form a more vibrant and dynamic personality.

The Cosmic Recipe

To summarize, think of the primary, secondary, and supportive chakra types as a constellation or blueprint. In general, this blueprint represents how the universe's profound intelligence has instilled specific forces within you and orchestrated their interaction, enabling you to fulfill your soul's purpose in this lifetime. The universe granted you your essence—your primary chakra—a unique aspect of life that constitutes your individual experience. This essence represents your true nature: what you are destined to embody and live.

Graciously, the universe's profound intelligence also provided you with a means to express yourself, allowing you to fulfill your essence. Your secondary chakra type is a conduit or structure through which you can channel your essence. And, in its limitless generosity, the universe bestowed upon you a source of strength, known as the supportive chakra. You draw energy from your supportive chakra type, which allows you to advance on your journey so that you can achieve your potential and manifest your essence. After all, this is a demanding voyage that requires a form of fuel or empowerment.

Hence, one might say that a chakra blueprint encapsulates the who, what, and how. In a similar vein, your blueprint can be likened to a cosmic recipe. Imagine preparing an exquisite dish and then sprinkling in spices that either amplify its flavors or mellow them.

As you examine your chakra blueprint, observe which chakras do not make an appearance in your configuration. This, too, is valuable and intriguing data. Be curious about what is present in your blueprint *and* what is absent, because you must learn to adjust your system in such a way that you occasionally recognize the traits that don't come naturally to you. These are not traits that you are intended to inherently possess. Quite often, people instinctively absorb these missing qualities from others. For instance, you may form relationships with individuals who mirror your composition to a certain extent, yet they also bring in an element entirely absent from your own blueprint; in this way, they help you achieve a sense of wholeness that couldn't be accomplished on your own. However, the challenge in relationships arises when you overlook this remarkable aspect. Instead of expressing gratitude to your partner for enriching your life—for instance, saying, "Thank you for adding the root chakra to my life!"—you may turn critical and judgmental, thereby missing out on a wonderful opportunity to receive these gifts that ultimately complete your chakra constellation. If you can't obtain these missing qualities from others, you can still acquire them through your personal development and efforts to attain balance.

Remember, the transformative journey of chakra types begins with self-acceptance. You can't morph into something you're not, and you can't fabricate a new version of yourself. However, you can evolve and grow without denying your authentic self. Embrace who you are and, grounded in this compassion, ensure that you don't harm yourself by indulging in your own excesses. Maintaining equilibrium is also a manifestation of self-love, isn't it?

Upon positioning all three chakra types appropriately, you'll finally be prepared to delve into your blueprint and interpret it. As pointed out earlier, it's remarkable how much insight can be gleaned from merely examining three figures. A simple glance at a combination such as 6–5–3 is all it takes to draw a myriad of conclusions.

FOUR

TOOLS FOR THE SOUL

This chapter introduces three techniques to help you determine your soul design. The questionnaire and the descriptions of the seven chakra types have probably given you some idea of your dominant chakras, but you might still be figuring out the exact order of your primary, secondary, and supportive types. Revisiting the questionnaire a couple of times and reviewing the descriptions of the seven types can be beneficial. You could also keep a journal and observe your interactions and responses in daily situations. This introspective journey can significantly boost your self-awareness, reshaping how you view yourself and those around you.

The three techniques in this chapter are designed to significantly refine your blossoming self-awareness. They aim to equip you with a richer understanding of your life's experiences and overarching themes. Often, people remain unaware of their innate connection with life, the fundamental way they experience and perceive their surroundings. Due to societal influences and conditioning, your connection to your primary chakra type can become clouded, distancing you from this foundational life experience. Accessing this deep-rooted aspect of self means delving into the heart of your perception, drawing you nearer to the essence of your primary chakra type.

Practice
● ● ● ● ● ● ●
UNCOVERING YOUR PRIMAL NARRATIVE

The primal narrative is one of the most profound tools for self-awareness that I'm aware of. This technique is designed to sharpen your discernment of your primary chakra type—the central point around which your secondary and supportive chakra types orbit. As touched upon earlier, there are two methods to understand your primary chakra type: one is through the lens of your life's core theme or primal narrative, and the other is via your most profound passions. Let's look at the essence of the core narrative.

Every individual grapples with the world in their own way. This persistent tension often traces back to your earliest memories. This core narrative emerges from your fundamental experiences in life, dictating how you engage and resonate with the world around you. Think of it as the dynamic between the "self" and the "world" and the subsequent challenges this brings. Consider your aspirations and the way they're thwarted by external circumstances or people, as well as your quest for fulfillment that, at times, is met with rejection and denial, and may even lead to hopelessness.

Your ongoing internal battles can be compared to the structure of a tree. The core struggle forms the trunk, whereas the countless minor conflicts you encounter resemble the branches and leaves. By digging into the trunk and its roots and confronting your fundamental narrative head-on, you can modify or even revolutionize the essence of your life's challenges.

The captivating aspect of this internal battle is its foundational presence in you. Although it manifested during your earliest memories, its inherent nature—thus, the term "primal"—suggests that many of your initial encounters simply validated deep-seated feelings you already had. This often leads to thoughts like *I some-*

how anticipated that this would culminate in disappointment and that loyalty would be fleeting.

The primal narrative functions as an ingrained lens that shapes how you interpret and narrate your life's journey. To truly grasp this narrative, try finishing the phrase: "As far back as I can recall, I've always felt that…" What underlying emotions or challenges arise from this reflection? By pinpointing your primal narrative, you begin to align with the core tension characteristic of your primary chakra type.

How can you unearth your primal narrative? Well, it's deeply embedded in how you recount your life's journey. Note: You might have recounted your life story many times before. It's essential to recognize that as you progress on your journey, you will continually unearth previously unexplored layers of your narrative. With each challenge, you are nudged to delve deeper or refine your understanding of life's tale. So, approach your story with fresh eyes, setting aside past conclusions and revelations. Share it as you genuinely feel it in the present moment, understanding that unveiling your primal narrative is an ever-evolving process.

Set aside about thirty minutes for this exercise.

Narrate

1. Close your eyes. Take deep, rhythmic breaths, allowing each exhalation to deepen your relaxation. Immersed in this tranquility, revisit your life's journey, from its start to the present. Begin to pin down your life story, capturing its essence as you currently perceive and feel it. Avoid a piecemeal approach such as "I grew up here, then attended school there." Instead, aim to weave your life into a coherent narrative, one that connects every event with a common thread, highlighting a primary theme, challenge, or direction. Concentrate on your soul's desires, the ambitions it has chased, and the obstacles you've encountered. When recounting your story, don't aim to dazzle or impress; this isn't about showcasing a series of triumphs. Instead, approach your narrative with authenticity,

highlighting the recurring challenges you've faced and the ways you've navigated the core trials in your life.

2. Reflect on the events and influences that had the most significant impact on your personality. When considering the timeline of your life, can you pinpoint a prevailing theme or direction? How would you articulate the journey of your growth into the person you are today? Capture the dominant sentiment of your narrative. What emotion does your story predominantly evoke? What primary thought emerges from it? If you were to encapsulate the essence of your story in a headline, what would it be?

If you are struggling to complete your narrative, I recommend beginning by recounting your earliest memories from childhood. Complete the following sentences: "From my youngest years, my foundational experience of life was…" or "Between the ages of seven and twelve, my fundamental feelings about life were…" These are the years in which the primal narrative begins to emerge. You may also consider the following questions:

- Can you recall your initial setbacks? Were they linked to a profound wish that went unfulfilled?
- What set you apart from your peers?
- Can you recall instances of feeling strong or vulnerable during your younger years?

Reflect

Reflecting on your narrative, ponder the following:

3. How did you opt to narrate your story, and from which vantage point? Which aspects seemed most pivotal to you? Did you place emphasis on certain elements over others?

4. Which facets of your story stood out and received the most attention? You may have highlighted achievements and setbacks, or you may have spotlighted relationships or a spiritual

odyssey. This reflection serves as a mirror of your intrinsic values.

5. Can you identify the core tension that runs through your narrative?

6. What motivations or reasons underpinned the decisions and actions you took in your story?

7. Is there a central theme or common thread that ties together your life's narrative?

Practice
YOUR LIFE EXPERIENCE

In the last exercise, you explored how you perceive life through the lens of aspirations and challenges. In other words, you considered the pursuit of your desires and how they sometimes conflicted with reality. In this exercise, you'll continue to deepen your self-awareness. You'll shift your focus to a cheerier aspect: connecting with the elements that best define your primary type—your passions, innate tendencies, and sources of happiness and meaning.

What constitutes a person's way of experiencing life? Often, we're not wholly conscious of our personal perceptions. Occasionally, in candid moments with a friend, you may find yourself saying something like, "You always view things in this way or react like that. I'm different; I approach situations this way..." These offhand remarks hint at your unique way of perceiving and interacting with the world. This individual perspective shapes how you interpret events, what captures your attention, what you dismiss or neglect, and how you discern between experiences that resonate with you and those that feel trivial.

Consider it this way: between you and the world exists a distinct gap or interval. Within this space, there lies the intrinsic way that you react, respond, and absorb information, which is truly individual. Now, your aim is to dive into this space and explore its intricacies.

This exercise is divided into two segments. The first segment includes ten prompts, some reminiscent of the earlier question-naire. This similarity isn't coincidental, as I designed several of the questionnaire's queries to help you delve into and articulate your individual life experiences. In this exercise, though, there are no multiple-choice questions. Instead, you're encouraged to let your thoughts flow freely, so be mindful of your written reflections.

These questions aim to heighten your awareness of how you interpret life's journey: your insights on its purpose and the oppor-tunities it presents to you and to each of us. Although we all reside on the same planet, our perceptions of it vary. Each individual's focuses and values differ; it's as though each of us inhabits different worlds. Recognize this crucial fact: what brings each of us to life is unique.

As you read through this exercise's reflection questions, delve deep into your genuine experiences, bypassing what you believe is the "correct" response or what matches your external persona. Instead, focus on your heartfelt emotions. Reflect on how you perceive your relationship with the world and the primary ways you've engaged with it since childhood. Rather than dwelling on conflicts or disconnects, concentrate on the essence of your rela-tionship with the world.

Set aside any thoughts of the questionnaire. Approach these questions with an open heart and mind, allowing for unexpected revelations. Tune in to your core values, those principles you regard as significant, commendable, and deserving of reverence. Remem-ber, values aren't universal. Contemplate the experiences that fill you with joy and fulfillment. Discern your unique brand of hap-piness, looking beyond universally celebrated moments like wed-dings or the birth of a child. Instead, search for those experiences that resonate and illuminate what happiness truly means for you.

Reflect

Don't feel compelled to address each of these prompts. Instead, view them as stimulants for reflection. You're free to approach them in any order—whether sequentially, from the middle, or even backward. The goal is to look deeply at your fundamental perceptions and your innate connection with existence.

Allot about twenty minutes for this segment of the exercise.

1. How do you interpret life's journey? What's your purpose, in terms of the opportunities this existence presents? Is it genuine self-expression? Forging bonds and expressing love? Unraveling life's enigmas? Spiritual enlightenment?

2. How do you see yourself in relation to the world? Finish this sentence: "Since my early years, I've primarily engaged with the world by…"

3. Which facet of your being feels most alive? Is it your analytical mind, your thirst for knowledge, or your intellectual prowess? Or perhaps it's your inclination toward meditation? Are you driven by your emotions, passions, or intense feelings? What truly embodies your essence?

4. Finish this sentence: "At my core, I am a…"

5. Finish this sentence: "Moments that truly invigorate me are when…"

6. Finish this sentence: "Values I hold closest to my heart include…"

7. Which situations or moments bring you the most joy and satisfaction?

8. Conversely, reflect on situations that cause you distress or sorrow. What diminishes your joy?

9. What first stands out when you meet people, and which facet of yourself readily interacts with your surroundings? Are you led by your analytical side? Your emotions? Do you often form judgments or seek to forge connections? Are you inclined toward intuitive insights or visionary thoughts?

10. Finish this sentence: "The primary focus of my thoughts often pertains to…" (relationships, career pursuits, spiritual reflections, academic endeavors, etc.). Recognizing where your

mind tends to wander offers insight into what truly holds significance for you.

Shift

Now, you are going to reapproach these questions from a different perspective.

Set aside ten to fifteen minutes for the introspective portion of this exercise.

11. I would like you to step into the shoes of someone you're close to who is quite different from you. Select someone whose life experiences you're familiar with, but who often sees the world in a way that diverges from your perspective; at times, you might even find their viewpoint challenging to empathize with, given the stark differences. This could be your partner, a friend, a family member, a coworker, or even your child.

12. Consider a personal challenge you're facing. How would it appear through that person's lens? How might you tackle this issue while embracing their perspective—a viewpoint you wouldn't typically adopt?

While this exercise seems deceptively simple, endeavor to truly unearth both your core beliefs and those of the other person. This can help you in two ways. First, by comparing these specific life experiences, you can clearly see the unique ways you view and interact with the world. This understanding will help you confidently connect with your primary chakra type. Second, it's often difficult to genuinely acknowledge that another's experience is just as valid as yours. This exercise aims to bridge that gap, urging you to connect deeply with another's point of view, not just in thought, but in feeling. Dive into their lived experiences as if they were your own and relish the chance to understand a different inner world. The chakra types system also underscores the importance of acceptance, teaching you to value and appreciate the myriad ways people perceive and engage with the world.

Practice

• • • • • •

BEING YOUR TYPE

This exercise is designed to help you separate who you truly are from who you believe you should be. This distinction is vital for fully embracing and aligning with your primary chakra type. When you are in harmony with your primary chakra, things naturally stabilize. This clarity will make it easier to identify your secondary and supportive chakra types, providing greater clarity to your overall blueprint. That's why pinpointing your primary chakra is always the starting point.

This journey starts with acceptance. First, you need to discover what you're actually accepting. It's important to connect with your true self, not the version of you that has been influenced by society's expectations. With so many external ideas in your mind, following advice like "Just be yourself" or "Relax and be who you are" can be tricky. You need to really understand what this advice means before you can follow it.

Over time, both consciously and subconsciously, you've built a self-image that might not truly represent your genuine self. This image is often tailored to what you think others might admire, endorse, or validate. It's your societal persona. The challenge lies in the fact that your authentic identity and this constructed self can become so deeply intertwined that distinguishing between them is difficult.

To gain clarity, undertake this simple exercise.

Construct

1. Create two columns on a piece of paper. Label the right one "The Real Me." This column represents the raw, unaltered person you genuinely are, devoid of societal expectations and imaginations. Label the left column "The 'Should Be' Me," which embodies the version of yourself that is shaped by societal norms, expectations, external influences, perceptions of others, or societal standards. Influences are not always direct

guidance from parents, teachers, or friends, but more subtle cues from them and from society as a whole.

By setting up these two columns, you can visually discern the imagined self from your authentic essence. While one column reflects the societal expectations molding your persona, the other captures your genuine self or *soul print*. It's crucial to understand that aspects of your current identity may have been shaped by external influences.

2. Start with "The 'Should Be' Me" column. Not only is it simpler, but it also provides a clearer lens with which to discern your true self, which often contrasts these external perceptions.

Jot down all the self-perceptions you've formed and the expectations that you've integrated over time. Identifying these notions isn't challenging, as they often manifest in your recurring thoughts and hidden aspirations. They might sound like "I should be achieving more," "I ought to express more love," "I need to be more focused," or "I should demonstrate greater dedication." These factors often hinder your connection to your true self. If it aids your introspection, reflect on various dimensions of your life, like your behavior, daily routines, professional path, and romantic engagements.

It's equally vital to reflect on the aspects of yourself that you've been told to suppress or change. Often, these criticisms come from individuals with differing chakra orientations who, consciously or unconsciously, want you to align more with their values. Such feedback can fuel misunderstandings in relationships. Some common critiques include:

- "Why are you always so serious? Loosen up a bit" (suggesting that you should be more light-hearted and adaptable)
- "Must you be so emotional? Toughen up" (implying a need to be less sensitive and more resilient)

- "You're always buried in your books; live a little" (hinting at a desire for you to be less introspective and more carefree)
- "Your routine is stifling" (meaning you should be more spontaneous, free-flowing, and adventurous)
- "You seem so distant; be present" (implying you should be more practical, engaged, and attentive to life's small details)

External judgments often seep into the psyche, morphing into internal beliefs and creating distance from your genuine self. Leverage your understanding of your primary chakra type to enrich your self-awareness and interpret these messages more constructively.

3. After carefully completing the left-hand column, turn your attention to the right. Remember, the right-hand column should reflect insights from the left-hand one but with a neutral and compassionate perspective. Aim for genuine self-description, avoiding harsh or judgmental language.

For instance, if the left-hand column says, "I should stop feeling like a failure," resist the urge to write "I am a failure" on the right. This doesn't accurately represent your true self—it's merely a negative perception in disguise. Seek to recognize and portray your authentic self without criticism. For example, if the left-hand column states, "I should be lighter and go with the flow"—perhaps influenced by external voices—your authentic self might resonate with "I value stability and deliberate action." This isn't a judgment; it's an acknowledgment of your nature. If the left-hand column says, "I should not be so attached emotionally," an objective self-reflection might be "I develop emotional attachments quickly." Again, this is a genuine observation, not a critique. As you rephrase the statements in the left-hand column, you transition from perceived ideals to genuine self-descriptions.

Acknowledge

4. Take a moment to review the left-hand column, labeled "The 'Should Be' Me." Observe each item you've listed. As you contemplate these points, realize that such a person doesn't truly exist. This "Should Be" version of yourself is a construct, a mere figment of imagination. Understand that this perspective isn't aiding your growth. Imagine, just for a moment, who you might be in the absence of these "should be's," without these preconceived notions clouding your vision. It will become clear how much internal conflict you harbor.

   When you continually strive to change your very essence, it is akin to a tree wishing to become a butterfly. We universally acknowledge the beauty of trees, and if one were to express a desire to morph into a butterfly, we'd be baffled and reassure it of its inherent magnificence. Yet, when it comes to your own self-perception, you may fall victim to the delusion that you can, and should, adopt an entirely different nature. This is when the power of imagination is misleading. The power of imagination has a dual impact on life. One facet of it sparks creativity, giving birth to animated films, enthralling novels, and boundless artistry. Yet there's another side to imagination, one that can estrange you from your true essence and the reality you inhabit. Your mission is to liberate yourself from this latter, limiting kind.

5. Now, shift your gaze to the right-hand column, designated as "The Real Me," and acknowledge its authenticity. See your genuine self clearly, free of embellishments. If you'd like, you can rename "The Real Me" column to "The 'Should Be' Me." This signifies that you are exactly as you should be, right here and now. Embrace this revelation. Recognize that this essence of yours is the universe's profound wisdom—the same force that crafted black holes, supernovas, ants, trees, mountains, and intricate molecules. Your only true task is to affirm your inherent nature. Then, rather than attempting to alter or replace your essence, you can nurture it and grow within its framework.

When I fully settle into my authentic self, I instantly feel an interconnectedness with everything. Think of yourself as a unique puzzle piece in the vast puzzle of the universe. Once you find your rightful place within this puzzle, the bigger picture becomes evident, and everything feels aligned. This profound sense of belonging and alignment is your cosmic connection.

Every archetype, including your specific chakra blueprint, comes with its limits and excesses. You may oscillate between extremes, either wholly accepting your nature with a resigned "This is who I am" or fervently wishing for transformation. This dichotomy is a pitfall that you must avoid. Do not overlook the existence of a middle ground.

Balance emerges from a profound relaxation into your true self, an affirmation that you don't necessarily need drastic change. If you are a Thinker and you tend to be arrogant, recognize and embrace it. Once you've genuinely accepted yourself, you're free to evolve. This growth doesn't negate your initial acknowledgment—it stems from it. It's a harmonious progression, devoid of inner turmoil or fanciful notions. When you are rooted in deep awareness, you allow your intrinsic self to blossom.

Visualize

As you approach this final stage, take a deep breath and immerse yourself in introspection.

6. Whether through writing, meditating, or visualizing, contemplate the following question: How would your life transform if you genuinely and passionately embraced your chakra type?

7. In your mind's eye, picture living a life where you embrace your chakra type without reservations. Push aside concerns of imbalances or excesses related to your chakra type, and know that growth is a continuous journey. Immerse yourself in this introspection. How would such an approach resonate in your physical sensations, emotions, thoughts, and overall presence?

PART II
FIND YOUR ANSWERS

FIVE

INTERPRETING YOUR CHAKRA DESIGN

As you continue on the journey of discerning your chakra types, the next step is deciphering your cosmic blueprint. Your quest is to fathom how the vast cosmos forged this distinct combination—the very combination that led to your inherent personality. After you have tackled the questionnaire, immersed yourself in the various chakra types, and undertaken the practices in chapter 4, your three dominant chakras should emerge.

Interestingly, your chakra blueprint is distilled into just three numbers. These numbers correspond with the chakra's position in the central channel. For example, the root chakra is represented by the number 1, the sacral chakra by the number 2, and so on. A glance at your blueprint might reveal patterns like 1–3–4 or 5–6–2. It might seem simplistic at first blush, yet the heart of this book is dedicated to unveiling the richness contained within these three numbers. Their depth is so layered that they command a significant portion of the discussion.

In this chapter, we'll explore the unique roles and meanings of the primary, secondary, and supportive chakra types. Each has its distinct function. When combined within the triad structure, they paint a captivating portrait shaped by their interrelations. These chakras operate individually, but there's a complex interaction among them, reflecting their balancing and empowering dynamics. The more deeply you explore your blueprint, the more you will appreciate its beauty—the beauty mirroring your personality. However, this design is also a cradle of conflicts and contradictions. It's crucial to discern both the allure and the imbalances.

Your chakra blueprint provides more than just insight into each chakra's function, such as how you find fulfillment or the source of your empowerment. It also unveils critical aspects like inherent frictions and tensions, especially those between the primary and secondary chakras. It illuminates which elements of your being are immutable, potential pitfalls to avoid to prevent self-destruction, and what naturally brings (or could bring) balance to you. Furthermore, this blueprint helps you discern your intrinsic nature. Are you more active or passive? Do you resonate with potent or soft energies? Are you grounded, or do you tend to drift? Do your tendencies lean toward being cool, warm, or perhaps fiery in nature?

In chapter 6, you'll dive into the intricacies of blueprint reading, starting with your own. You'll decode specific combinations and uncover the depth within these three pivotal numbers. To truly understand a blueprint, be it yours or another's, patience is key. All three dominant chakras must find their place within the constellation before you can interpret their meaning. It's vital to savor this journey, as it can be a therapeutic and introspective form of self-coaching. While I don't expect you to undergo a major shift in your identity (your conclusions from part I will likely remain consistent), the journey of self-discovery often has surprises. If changes do emerge, they'll likely be subtle shifts within the triad itself. For instance, you might discover that what you once perceived as your primary chakra type resonates more as a secondary type, or perhaps your supportive type feels more akin to a secondary one. Discerning the structure of your three dominant chakras often demands the most introspection and time.

As you delve deeper into interpreting your blueprint, the relationship between the various facets of your personality will crystallize. In the process, you might sense that certain aspects do not resonate with you. This insight allows you to fine-tune your understanding. After all, your blueprint should seamlessly align with your essence, providing answers to your most profound questions.

As part of this journey toward self-identification, chapter 7 will briefly discuss the forty-two possible combinations of the primary and secondary chakra types. As you explore these combinations, you'll gain a richer understanding of how the primary and secondary chakras intertwine. You might even find a type that mirrors your inner essence, further facilitating self-realization. These forty-two combinations detail primary sources of happiness and meaning, but it's essential to remember that when factoring in the supportive chakra, the spectrum expands to a staggering 210 personality types!

Next, we'll explore each of the three chakra types in detail and illuminate the intricate relationships between them.

Meaning and Role of the Primary Chakra Type

The primary chakra type represents the heart of your personality and is deeply connected to the very essence of your soul and its journey. Hence, I term it the "soul print," symbolizing the soul's presence within.

Your primary chakra type serves as the main conduit through which you perceive and engage with life. While we all tap into a range of emotions, thoughts, sensations, and instincts, there is a predominant pathway that is uniquely yours. Envision the primary chakra as the sun, with the supportive and secondary chakra types orbiting around it like planets.

The primary chakra type resonates with your innermost desires and inclinations. It illuminates what truly satisfies your heart's yearnings and makes you feel aligned with your true self. Understanding this chakra helps reveal what brings you genuine happiness and imbues your life with meaning. It's essential to recognize that what fulfills one person may not satisfy another. Consider this: What would you passionately pursue without any expectations of reward or recognition? How can you feel deeply connected to the world, as if there's no barrier between you and the vast expanse of life? This profound connection and joy will undoubtedly be what you'll want to share with the world. When you drift from this central passion, life will become marked by discontent and a sense of emptiness. Feeling unsatisfied, sensing a hunger in your soul, or feeling out of place are strong indicators that you've strayed from your primary chakra type.

When you deviate from your primary chakra type and lean into your secondary or supportive types, it can lead to feelings of disorientation. These secondary and supportive types, though important, don't provide the same foundation of happiness and purpose. Adopting their values can create internal conflict, knocking things out of balance. The push to realign with your primary chakra is a natural sign. However, being drawn to the secondary or supportive chakras is understandable given their strong influence. Such transitions are part of your journey, but it's essential to recognize them and restore balance swiftly.

The primary chakra type, given its central importance, also defines your main challenges or conflicts in life. Why? Simply put, what connects you to life can also be what separates you from it, especially when those connections are strained. Consider someone with a primary throat chakra: their strongest connection with life may be through influencing and bringing transformative visions to those around them. But when this is hindered, they might resort to controlling or manipulative behaviors. This very inability to achieve what the heart desires most becomes a significant challenge. It's a natural human response.

When the primary chakra type manifests as a dominant personality trait, it becomes a hyper-focused lens through which you experience life, concentrating intently on one aspect. However, life often pushes back against this narrow perspective, seeking to enrich and diversify your experiences. For example, if you predominantly operate from the sixth chakra, focusing solely on intellectual observation, life will challenge this by suggesting that there is so much more to embrace. Yet Thinkers might resist this broadening. This resistance and interaction between your primary chakra and life's challenges create the overarching theme of your existence.

You may sometimes feel the challenges of your secondary chakra as if they were your primary battles. This often arises from over-associating with your secondary chakra type, causing you to lose sight of your primary chakra. It's essential to realize that while your secondary chakra aids in fulfillment, it isn't your true essence. Overcomplicating your life by adding unnecessary conflicts is not the goal—you already have ample challenges to navigate.

For this reason, I constantly emphasize a key solution: always anchor yourself in your primary chakra type. This is your true center, especially when you are seeking connection with your intrinsic sources of joy and purpose. The primary chakra type represents self-acceptance at its core. To genuinely embrace yourself, you must first recognize and align with your primary chakra type.

When equilibrium is found between the primary and secondary chakras, it's a moment of genuine triumph. You've reached a pinnacle of inner harmony and profound self-awareness.

Once you anchor yourself in the primary chakra type, you'll naturally wonder, *Now that I know my essence, what tools will bring me fulfillment? How can I harness my potential and find support?* Imagine the secondary and supportive relationships as the bond between a driver and their vehicle. In this analogy, your secondary chakra type is the destination you are moving toward, while your supportive chakra type is the vehicle propelling you forward. It's the driving force that transitions you from A to B, but always remember, your essence is in the driver's seat.

The primary chakra type shapes your constitution, be it energetic or calm. This inherent nature can be intensified or harmonized depending on the influence of the other two types. While not every chakra configuration includes a balancing element, there's often a stabilizing factor present, a gift from the universe's benevolence.

Meaning and Role of the Secondary Chakra Type

The secondary chakra plays a pivotal role in shaping your external persona, although it is not as defining as your primary chakra type. Your secondary chakra type might not represent your core values or dictate your happiness and sense of purpose, but it profoundly influences your action, manifestation, and expression.

Envision the primary chakra type as the subtle core within. The secondary chakra type illuminates your essence so that it shines outwardly. You have innate passions that steer you toward joy and purpose, and you also have a distinct way of expressing yourself in the world. If your secondary type is the root, solar plexus, or throat chakra, you're endowed with a powerful capacity for manifestation. Being a Builder, Achiever, or Speaker emphasizes the manifesting strength rooted in these pivotal chakras, providing the robust foundation for your true self to flourish. In contrast, if your secondary type is that of an Artist (sacral), Caretaker (heart), Thinker (third eye), or Yogi (crown), your outward expression leans less toward tangible manifestation. Such a disposition might make you seem detached or ethereal, especially when judged by societal standards that emphasize productivity, ambition, and discipline. These secondary chakras bring a sense of openness and buoy-ancy. However, this doesn't suggest an inability to create. It means that you're more attuned to elements like the emotional fluidity of the sacral or heart chakras, or the airy qualities of the third eye and crown, rather than the fiery nature of the solar plexus and throat chakras or the groundedness of the root chakra. These elemental associations will be discussed in detail in chapter 6, as they are pivotal to understanding.

Embracing such a constitution may be a pivotal moment in the journey toward self-acceptance. It teaches you to detach from societal standards and appreciate your unique constitution. If you discover that your essence leans toward the airy aspect of the third eye chakra, for example, your focus is not on changing this facet of your personality but on appreciating its inherent beauty.

When your primary chakra type resonates with the elements of air and water (represented by the sacral, heart, third eye, and crown chakras) and is complemented by a secondary chakra type of similar elements, your trajectory may not include tangible achievements or self-fulfillment. This doesn't reduce your inherent talents; it just hints that you might benefit from some external support. Such backing could come from a structured environment or even col-laborative partnerships that bolster your sense of direction, aiding your for-ward motion. The supportive energy of the solar plexus chakra, for example, can offer a harmonizing effect. However, relying purely on the throat or root chakras for support might be insufficient. To infuse such a system with its own purpose and drive, the fiery essence of the third chakra is indispensable.

Understanding the idea of expression is essential in today's world. At its core, expression is about manifesting your true self. It's the medium through which your authenticity shines in the world. This manifestation doesn't always need to be intense or overt. Each individual has a unique way of harnessing and manifesting their inner potential. For some, this might be through relationships, especially if they resonate with the energy of the heart chakra. For others, it might be through a spiritual journey, aligning with the energy of the crown chakra. Thus, it's crucial to expand your perspective on what fulfillment truly means.

Your secondary chakra type can sharpen the focus of your primary chakra, much like an arrow precisely aimed at a target. For example, if you identify primarily with the Caretaker type and pair it with the Speaker, your primary type's direction becomes more defined. The same applies if your primary type is the Achiever and your secondary is the Builder. In such combinations, the elemental fire within you is amplified.

Conversely, certain combinations can introduce a cooling effect, making one's life journey feel more serene and gentle. However, this openness can also lead to uncertainty. It means that the clear, burning passion about one's purpose or destiny might not be as evident. This explains why some individuals have a crystal-clear vision of their path, while others adopt a more explorative approach to life.

Again, we will discuss this elemental energy in more detail in the next chapter.

Meaning and Role of the Supportive Chakra Type

The supportive chakra type can be succinctly described as a dominant chakra within you. While it might not align with your core values or dictate your outward manifestations, it plays a pivotal role in balancing and propelling your entire system. Think of it as a guiding force that nudges the system in a specific direction. On its own, the supportive type provides the strength, nourishment, and empowerment that enables the primary and secondary chakra types to pursue their passions, find meaning, and achieve true happiness. Essentially, it acts as a power source for your life's purpose. However, this perspective requires you to consider the supportive chakra type separately from the entire system. Then, when the supportive chakra type is incorporated into the overall system, its effect is transformative, shifting the balance and interplay of energies in a significant way. This chakra type profoundly affects your energetic makeup and can alter the proportions of fire, air, water, or earth elements within you.

Consider a supportive type that resonates with fiery energy, such as the root, solar plexus, or throat chakras. Depending on the primary and secondary chakra types present, this supportive chakra type could amplify a fiery temperament, potentially leading to harmful imbalances; enhance one's capacity to bring ideas to life; or stabilize a blueprint dominated by water or air elements, lending it clarity and purpose. For instance, someone with a primary sacral chakra and secondary heart chakra embodies watery and airy energies. But if the throat chakra was their supportive chakra type, it would infuse this ethereal individual with a sense of aspiration and manifestation and introduce a fiery essence.

Naturally, some chakras aren't inherently fiery in nature, such as the root chakra or the third eye chakra. However, when positioned within a specific energetic constellation, their intensity can be amplified. This adaptability is what makes them intriguing. Depending on the overall blueprint, these chakras can either modify their attributes or accentuate certain areas within the constellation.

Certain chakra systems inherently maintain equilibrium, while others need a bit more attention to find that balance or to be strengthened. If you find yourself overly intense, seek harmony. On the other hand, if you lean toward being too light or too fluid, it's time to harness your inner power. Don't lose heart if your system requires more effort to stabilize! Such a path often adds a layer of mystique and wonder. I sometimes observe blueprints that are predominantly airy or watery, but the inherent beauty and the gifts each blueprint brings are undeniable.

Here are two crucial insights regarding blueprints. First, examining the blueprint and its interactions can reveal whether or not a person is innately a warm and emotional being. Some people are distant or indifferent to human emotions and relationships, while others exude warmth and are deeply emotional. If you recognize a lack of emotional depth within yourself, this can be counteracted in various ways. One method is through forming bonds with those who overflow with the emotions you lack, thus fostering balance. Alternatively, you could cultivate an environment that soothes your soul or embark on a journey of introspection and personal growth, which is invariably rewarding.

Second, your blueprint isn't a direct indicator of your potential talent in a given field. Being a throat chakra type, a Speaker, combined with a sacral chakra type, an Artist, doesn't necessarily mean you'll become the most renowned musician in history. The chakra blueprint system doesn't operate on that premise. However, while your blueprint might not pinpoint specific talents, it can certainly highlight foundational elements that will nurture your inherent potential.

Furthermore, the system isn't a tool to predict whether you'll wield it for good or ill. However, certain elements within can suggest predispositions toward disruptive tendencies. A particularly fiery system can be seen as riskier due to its heightened energy, passion, and inherent potential for destruction. Yet, when this immense energy is channeled effectively, it has the power to revolutionize the world!

Practice
· · · · · · ·
TAPPING INTO YOUR SECONDARY AND SUPPORTIVE CHAKRAS

By now, based on the questionnaire, the seven chakra type descriptions, and the exercises in part I, you likely have a solid grasp of your primary chakra type, and possibly your secondary type as well. However, pinpointing the supportive chakra type can be a bit elusive. To assist in this endeavor, I've crafted an exercise that builds on "Uncovering Your Primal Narrative," where you used your life story to identify your primary chakra. Telling your life story is immensely insightful, as how and what you emphasize reveals a lot about your inner makeup and the chakras that are dominant in your blueprint.

Narrate

In a moment, you are going to write down the narrative of your life, but in this exercise, I want you to bypass the quest for the primal narrative. Instead, let these guiding questions shape your story. They'll lead you to a distinct version of your life story, emphasizing your decision-making, the source of your drive, your triumphs over hurdles, and the realization of your dreams.

These five questions are carefully chosen to help you unearth your unique constellation. While these questions provide a structure, you don't need to rigidly follow them in sequence; you might occasionally refer to them as you narrate, or you may prefer a more systematic approach. Trust whichever method feels instinctive, as it's likely a reflection of your inherent constellation!

Allocate roughly thirty minutes to this segment of the exercise before moving on to the next phase of introspection.

1. Begin your introspection from your early years, journeying through adolescence and into your adult life. **How did your values set you apart from others? Contemplate how your beliefs diverged from those of your family, community, classmates, and friends.** In which aspects did you deviate from the norm? What were the driving forces behind your choices? What influenced your thoughts, feelings, and actions, be they your career decisions or your firm beliefs about justice, truth, or righteousness? Pay special attention to how you differed from your family, perhaps even contrasting with siblings or parents, and extend this to your wider circle of community, classmates, and friends. This introspection is quite revealing in terms of the primary chakra type; it can shed light on your value system, what you prioritize, and your unique interpretation of happiness.

2. **What do you regard as your most significant accomplishment in life?** This question is closely linked to your secondary chakra type. Your most cherished achievement might not align with society's conventional benchmarks—this question asks what *you* personally view as the pinnacle of your achievements. This reflection is pivotal, as it illuminates your perception of true fulfillment and genuine realization.

3. **What did you yearn to become, even if those aspirations never materialized? What dreams did you hold dear, regardless of whether they became a reality? Why were these particular aspirations and dreams significant?** This question digs deeper into your secondary chakra type. Throughout the phases of your life—as a child, teenager, young adult, and perhaps even later—what were the dreams and visions you had for your future self and life's path? Even if life's challenges and setbacks altered these dreams, what were they? Moreover, don't neglect this crucial sub-question: "Why were these particular aspirations and dreams significant?" For instance, if you aspired to be a politician, investigate the reasoning behind this. Was it due to the career's significance, its potential to impact lives, or the

ability to shape laws? If it was the latter, you could delve into why crafting laws was so appealing. Explore the depths of your motivations.

4. **What sustained and invigorated you on your journey? From where did you draw your strength and vitality?** This question helps you tap into your supportive chakra type. Consider the wellsprings of your determination and spirit—those factors that propelled you forward, reignited your enthusiasm, and prevented you from giving up. Where did you find the energy that consistently supported and inspired you?

5. **Which three traits empowered you to surmount challenges in your path?** This final question aligns with the supportive type. While you can certainly list more than three core qualities, identify at least three that aided you during trying times, especially when the odds seemed insurmountable.

Reflect

While writing your life story through the lens of the previous five questions, you might have reinforced prior insights or perhaps gained clearer understandings.

6. Now, examine your narrative. Start by identifying which chakras seem absent in your recounting. Which chakra themes, values, or topics are noticeably overlooked in your narrative? Recognizing what's missing from your story can also help define your constellation. It's not that you can't resonate with the themes of these absent chakras—after all, you've navigated various themes in your life. But consider what wasn't accentuated as you answered these questions.

7. The five questions were merely guides, and while they might not correlate directly to a single chakra, they are effective in helping you discern your primary, secondary, and supportive types. Reflect on your response to the first question. How does it align with what you believe is your primary chakra type? Which chakra embodies the values you've described?

Does this align with your earlier understanding of your primary type?

8. Do your responses to the second and third questions align with what you've identified as your secondary chakra type? It's possible for these questions to resonate with the supportive type, occasionally highlighting it more prominently. Reflect on your answers, especially regarding your life's proudest achievements and your aspirations. Which chakra resonates with these ambitions and goals? Does this insight match your previous understanding?

9. Reflect on your responses to the fourth and fifth questions. What insights do they provide regarding your supportive chakra type? While the three qualities mentioned in the fifth question aren't exclusive to the supportive chakra and may blend aspects from your primary, secondary, or supportive chakras, examine whether these qualities shed light on your supportive chakra type.

10. Lastly, zoom out and examine your entire narrative. Can you discern which chakras stand out most prominently in your descriptions? There might be varying degrees of significance; one chakra could be distinctly dominant, with the others acting as minor influences. Reflect on the prevalence of certain chakras and see if this aligns with or refines what you understood previously.

SIX

—

DECODING YOUR SOUL'S BLUEPRINT

In this chapter, you'll delve deeper into the intricacies of the three-type structure, and you'll explore how to interpret your blueprint. Interpretation involves understanding the connections between the three forces. In part III, you'll go beyond deciphering it—you'll also discover how to harness these insights to address life's questions, how to find your balance, and how to determine the best approach to specific challenges. However, the first step is to grasp how to interpret your own blueprint as well as others'.

Once you've crafted your blueprint, there are two methods to initiate its interpretation. The first method involves listing your types sequentially from left to right: start with your primary type, then the secondary, and finally the supportive. Alternatively, envision three concentric circles: the innermost represents the primary type, closest to the soul, followed by the secondary and then the supportive as the outermost circle. This visualization isn't merely a structural concept but an intuitive tool to facilitate your understanding.

Gearing Up for the Adventure Ahead

Let's begin to immerse ourselves in the art of chakra blueprint reading.

I understand that initially, it may seem like you're merely gazing at numbers. Yet these numbers have substance, and there's a vast world between them. Imagine your chakra blueprint as a reflection of the continuous dance of dynamics within your personality. By grasping the interplay among the three, you'll unlock profound insight into your unique blueprint as a reflection of your living soul.

Examining the blueprint of your three chakra types demands careful consideration. This process is not a superficial glance or a swift read. Reflect on the three numbers, drawing upon all you've learned about the types and chakras. Revisit the constellation repeatedly, digging deeper each time, seeking to better understand it.

There are nine fundamental questions that will guide your exploration. As this chapter draws to a close, you'll engage with these questions, first by examining two different blueprints and then by assessing your own. (An exhilarating endeavor, isn't it?) During these exercises, avoid making generalized or ambiguous remarks. Aim for detailed and exact observations, and seek out particular imbalances. Have faith in the wealth of insight awaiting discovery.

The concept of the primary chakra type has been established. While recognizing this type offers some insight, it's only a static snapshot. The true depth of understanding emerges when you consider how the primary chakra is affected and transformed by the presence of two additional chakras. When you observe a blueprint, the primary chakra type evolves from a mere archetype to a multifaceted, living personality, reflecting a unique individual.

When I begin to analyze the three numbers in a blueprint, I first acknowledge the interplay between the primary and the secondary chakra types. While the primary chakra type shapes an individual's perspective and experience of life, the secondary chakra type dictates their expression within the world. Moreover, the influence of the secondary type on the primary can be empowering, enhancing, or intensifying, or it can soothe and relax, occasionally to the point of lethargy. (This dynamic is explored in chapter 7.)

When assessing the primary and secondary types, an inherent tension emerges. Primary and secondary chakra types often exert force in opposing directions. At times, this dichotomy is so pronounced that it might make you question whether you possess a dual personality, as though you are two distinct individuals. Both forces are potent—at times almost equally so—leading them to pull you in two directions.

When you're caught between conflicting inner voices, it's often a reflection of the underlying tension between your primary and secondary chakra types. During such internal conflicts, reflect: "Which voice echoes my primary type, and which aligns with the secondary?" This introspection offers clarity. Choosing a voice can be challenging since both hold profound importance in your psyche and life. Always keep in mind that when faced with a decision, you should begin by listening to the voice of your primary chakra, as it represents your core essence and wellspring of satisfaction. Ultimately, the decision you make might not be solely influenced by your primary chakra's voice, but it's the initial guidance you should heed. This concept will be further explored in part III.

At this stage, I trust you've come to understand that there isn't inherently a "bad" or "good" chakra blueprint. Assessing your chakra blueprint is not about striking gold or feeling dismayed by an "imperfect" layout. Yes, some combinations present more hurdles than others, but any blueprint can be harmonious and uplifting or riddled with conflict and paradox. Ultimately, it's your perspective and level of consciousness that define the journey.

When examining your chakra blueprint, accepting a degree of imbalance is essential. You may be tempted to idealize a perfectly balanced constellation, but such fantasies can be counterproductive. Remember, a little imbalance is part of overall balance. In fact, these minor discrepancies often foster a constructive tension crucial for personal growth. So, when interpreting your blueprint, avoid a judgmental lens that seeks a flawless equilibrium. Instead, understand it as a vibrant, occasionally contrasting constellation that's beneficial in its own right.

Reading a Blueprint Energetically

Before going further, I want you to immerse yourself in the energy of your inner structure. Don't approach your blueprint with strictly intellectual understanding; experience its dynamism and life force. Contemplate its essence. How does it resonate within you? Feeling its vitality is paramount because your primary aim isn't just cognitive understanding, but a deeper energetic perception.

When chakra types intertwine, they can either amplify or mellow specific elements, primarily the four foundational ones: fire, water, air, and earth. Furthermore, they can strengthen or diminish qualities such as vigor or softness, dynamism or stillness, warmth or coldness. When examining a blueprint, discern its elemental character: Does it embody the fierceness of fire? What about the traits of air, water, or earth? It might even be a mix, like being mainly air tinged with fiery undertones, or predominantly earth complemented by air's nuances.

A dominant fire element suggests vibrant energy; the blueprint pulsates with fervor, defined by its forward momentum, compelling drive, and ambition. In contrast, the water element resonates with emotion, sensitivity, dedication, relationships, and an experiential nature, focusing on deep feelings, presence, and intimacy. The earth element signifies tactile sensations, groundedness, tangibility, and pragmatism, underlined by efficiency, diligence, and discipline. Lastly, the air element is epitomized by its ethereal nature, clarity, detachment, spirituality, and a deep immersion in ideas and visions.

Chakra Type	Element Amplified	Additional Notes
Seventh (Crown)	Water/Air	Enhances passive and introspective qualities
Sixth (Third Eye)	Fire/Air	Duality depends on combination
Fifth (Throat)	Fire/Air	Boosts intensity with airy and fiery qualities
Fourth (Heart)	Water	Enhances passive and introspective qualities
Third (Solar Plexus)	Fire	Increases intensity and potency
Second (Sacral)	Water	Enhances passive and introspective qualities
First (Root)	Earth	Combines with other chakras to modify elemental characteristics

When examining the elements within a blueprint, focus on the dynamics of activity versus passivity and the spectrum between cold and warmth. This is your foundational understanding. Notably, introducing the solar plexus chakra type into any system immediately amplifies its fiery, potent energy. This chakra acts as a catalyst, pushing the entire system in a more intense direction. Similarly, the incorporation of the throat chakra type also boosts intensity, though not as vigorously as the solar plexus type. While the throat chakra type also has airy qualities, its fiery aspects often provide a system with direction and fervor. Conversely, a blueprint with the sacral, heart, or crown chakra types will amplify the water and air elements, as well as the passive attributes. This results in a system that becomes more receptive, gentle, emotionally nuanced, and introspective.

Introducing the root chakra and the third eye chakra into specific constellations is fascinating because they act as chameleonlike entities, shifting their nature based on the surrounding structure. For example, when the root chakra is combined with the sacral, crown, or heart chakra types, it amplifies the earth element while emphasizing active attributes due to its grounding and pragmatic nature. Interestingly, its fiery and potent traits are accentuated even further when paired with the solar plexus, throat, and third eye types. Essentially, the root chakra anchors other energies, connecting them to earthly traits with varying intensities.

As for the third eye chakra type, its nature transforms dramatically based on its pairings. When combined with the solar plexus or throat chakra types, it exhibits a more fiery and dynamic demeanor, channeling a potent intellectual energy. This is also evident when it is paired with the root chakra type. However, when the third eye chakra is combined with the sacral, heart, or crown chakra types, it reveals a gentler side, exuding an airy essence. Its inherent duality means that either the air or fire element can be magnified, depending on the blueprint.

The Nine Fundamental Questions

In this chapter, you'll be integrating nine questions tailored to enhance any chakra blueprint reading. Let's clarify the significance and intention of each question.

1. **How does the blueprint manifest energetically?** What characterizes its energetic essence? This question evaluates aspects like active/passive, hot/cold, and effective/ineffective. "Effective" refers to a chakra

structure that is both productive and purposefully oriented, while "ineffective" indicates a lesser emphasis on direction and advancement. Are there harmonizing components, or do the chakras simply amplify each other? Alternatively, could the overall blend be too passive, to the extent of being lethargic or idle? Aim to discern a distinct energetic profile. Valuable insights can be gained by identifying what's lacking in the structure; discerning its gaps provides a more thorough comprehension of a blueprint's energetic essence.

2. **What emerges when the primary and secondary chakra types combine?** What unique personality materializes from this combination? What gifts might this blend bestow upon the world? How can this constellation contribute positively? Does it hint at specific career paths? What strengths and challenges arise from this union? At this juncture, focus solely on the primary and secondary chakra types.

3. Consider the interplay or possible friction between the primary and secondary chakra types. **How does the secondary chakra type complement the primary, and conversely, how might it challenge it?** Reflect on the range of emotions, both uplifting and challenging, that stem from this pairing. Once you've contemplated these two chakra types, introduce the supportive chakra type into your reflection. Question whether the dynamic becomes more complex with this addition. How does the supportive type influence the existing duo? Ultimately, consider how centering in the primary chakra type could alleviate any tension.

4. **What stands out as the benefits and remarkable attributes of this specific blueprint?**

5. **Which aspects of this constellation need to be acknowledged and embraced as unchangeable?** Realizing what isn't meant to be altered often provides profound insight.

6. **What are the potential risks or self-sabotaging tendencies inherent in this structure?**

7. Additionally, **what wisdom does this pattern offer?** Which crucial life lessons arise, and what knowledge should be sought in order to foster growth?

8. **How can the full potential of this blueprint be harnessed?** What core strengths can be infused into daily life, work, interpersonal relationships, and any challenges encountered?

9. How can a harmonious balance be achieved within this configuration, considering one's relationships, surroundings, engagements, and personal reflections? Primarily, **how can the interplay between the primary and secondary elements be stabilized?** Discerning which four chakra types are absent in the blueprint can be enlightening—they often reveal the true path to balance.

These nine prompts will serve as invaluable compasses that provide deep insight into your own and others' blueprints.

Let's Read Blueprints!

In this section, I will carefully interpret one blueprint and briefly look at another. The twist? The first blueprint is my own. My motive for offering a comprehensive look at my blueprint isn't self-exposure; it's to inspire you to bravely interpret your own blueprint. The second analysis is of a friend's blueprint. My ultimate aim is to highlight the depth of understanding that can be found in a blueprint, using just three numbers as a guide.

6–5–3

At first glance, this structure exudes a strong, dynamic energy. Its heightened activity stems from being exclusively made up of fire and air elements. Without any moderating, cooling forces, the sixth chakra absorbs intense energy from the others, amplifying its power. This results in heightened intellectual capacity, leadership, eloquence, and a relentless drive toward objectives. Such a blueprint is geared toward excellence, consistently propelling itself forward and upward.

What results from the combination of the sixth and fifth chakras, the primary and secondary chakras? In the next chapter, examples will underscore that when the throat chakra is the secondary chakra type, it indicates a teaching persona. Having the fifth chakra as the secondary chakra type suggests being called to instruction. This blueprint sketches out a philosopher, researcher, or educator's path. Such individuals are primed to nurture ideas and impart them.

The key interplay is this: while the sixth chakra incubates ideas, the fifth chakra has an inherent urge to share and educate. Given this dynamic, the greatest fulfillment is found in transmitting and imparting insights. In other words, within this framework, ideas demand external expression.

This pairing suggests a strong dedication to the process. With the sixth chakra as the primary type rather than the fifth, the focus shifts from mere dissemination of ideas. The third eye chakra engenders a unique thought process, one deeply rooted in comprehensive learning, emphasizing accuracy and profound knowledge. Essentially, it's about articulating with confidence after thorough understanding. The third eye chakra type, naturally clear-sighted, aims for structured thinking and offers polished theories. Such a synergy continuously generates a plethora of ideas and visions.

Consider the combination of the third eye and throat chakra types if they were perhaps supported by the sacral or crown chakra. This blend would result in an ethereal, dreamlike disposition, predominantly influenced by the air element, leaving the system somewhat unanchored and less capable of real-world manifestation. However, in this blueprint, the solar plexus chakra is the supportive type, and as such, the system gains the ability to pursue ambitions with determination, perseverance, and robust energy. This addition infuses a fiery element. Thus, the system evolves from merely conceiving ideas and visions to actualizing them. With the solar plexus chakra type's influence, life is not just about dreaming—it's about achieving. Dreams transition into tangible goals that are pursued with unwavering commitment. This configuration epitomizes an "effective" personality, one that actively contributes to the world.

The sixth chakra type generates ideas, while the fifth chakra type communicates them, creating an interplay between introspection and expression. A key strength of this alignment is the third eye chakra's detachment, which allows for consistent progress and the capacity to shed the past. Essentially, this is a chakra blueprint resistant to stagnation.

This structure values comprehension and forward momentum, minimizing emotional baggage and the propensity to dwell on regret. The drive for progress is fueled by intense passion. Furthermore, the synergy of the sixth and third chakras produces a distinct individuality. This bestows the individual with a remarkable resilience, virtually indomitable.

This configuration is notably restless and intense, lacking the calming influences of the sacral, heart, crown, and (crucially) root chakra. This absence results in a relentless push toward the future and its potential, which leads the individual to overlook life's finer details. Their impatience is palpable, and they have a high risk of burnout.

However, it's vital to recognize the dominance of the third eye chakra in this alignment. This is a chakra rooted in contemplation, idea development, research, and learning, which form the crux of its contentment. Thus, while the throat chakra suggests outward expression and success, this configuration's true essence lies in the pursuit of insight and knowledge, not influence or achievement.

The tension between the fifth and sixth types is amplified by the third's influence. The solar plexus and throat chakras consistently steer one toward leadership, vision, and an extroverted lifestyle. They're about public exposure and achievement. Conversely, the third eye chakra is introspective, drawn to contemplation, intellectual pursuits, and moments of solitude. This creates a scenario where the individual is caught between these contrasting forces. As a result, their identity as a teacher, influencer, or leader isn't fully realized due to an internal resistance against the fifth and third chakras' extroversion. (It's astonishing how much insight can be gained from these three numbers, and we're just scratching the surface!)

The third eye chakra type, which values depth and sophistication, resists simplifying its knowledge. It doesn't wish to cheapen its profound insights and aims to maintain its high standing. This personality—confident to the point of arrogance—is driven by a desire to remain refined. In contrast, the throat chakra type seeks to make complex ideas straightforward and universally accessible.

The sixth chakra type grapples with conveying its ideas succinctly, often because it's unsure of how to distill such profound insights. This leads to considerable frustration. While the fifth chakra type facilitates the articulation of these ideas, it's crucial to recognize the innate reluctance of the sixth type. Yet, the latter is aware that withholding such insights hampers their impact, especially since the fifth chakra represents the culmination of these inner revelations.

The dynamics of this structure are intriguing. Its inherent resistance might limit its external influence, resulting in a tempered presence in the world despite such intense energy. Rather than overwhelming charisma or influence, this blueprint's strength is its depth. The essence of this setup, as portrayed by the sixth type, is the pursuit and realization of knowledge. It's not geared toward building vast systems or organizations; its primary goal is the cultivation of knowledge.

Think about how this combination could achieve harmony. This is something you'll need to reflect on. At its foundation, there's the support of the right company and nurturing partnerships. This blueprint can get along with the root chakra type; however, its marked impatience and difference in energy compared to the root chakra make it a loose association. In contrast, the chakra types that can bring equilibrium are the sacral, the heart, and, to a certain extent, the crown. The most suitable collaborators and harmonizers are the sacral and heart chakra types, as they alleviate and tame intensity. Importantly, they embody a balanced middle ground without veering toward any extremes. Clearly, such a structure resonates with the third, fifth, and sixth chakra types. However, there's a certain reluctance or difficulty in fully embracing the solar plexus and throat chakra personalities. While these chakra types may work together, they don't necessarily bring balance to each other.

Another approach to harmony is seeking a serene natural environment. For this particular blueprint, bustling urban settings can be detrimental. Introducing such an intense, fiery system to a cityscape only amplifies its restlessness. Moreover, urban areas are not particularly suitable for third eye chakra types. They tend to struggle with crowds, vast spaces, and major events, as they crave ample silence for reflection and meditation.

What additional guidance might suit this combination? This one must be approached with caution. Advising the individual to dedicate themselves to meditation or to consistently seek serenity could miss the mark, as we all need to embrace our innate makeup. Thus, it's wise to gently propose the following: seek moments of meditation and quiet; find joy and embrace beauty, including scenic surroundings; and cultivate some personal bonds. This blueprint certainly benefits from a stabilizing routine, calling for a steady level of physical movement. They aren't destined to overly exert themselves, but neither can they fully avoid physical activity. They should focus on life's nuances; however, such suggestions ought to be adopted in moderation, serving to enhance life's fullness.

Recall that I highlighted the risk of burnout for this chakra blueprint. It's crucial to recognize that high-intensity configurations often find it hard to pause. When people say, "Take a break" or "Don't be so serious," it's challenging for them to comply. Hence, to prevent burnout, these individuals must be trained to spot early symptoms and know when to halt.

This system faces two threats of burnout. Mentally, the third eye chakra type tends to overanalyze and immerse itself in study, making it susceptible. Additionally, both the throat and solar plexus chakra types risk burnout, with the solar plexus being particularly vulnerable due to its ceaseless activity and unwavering dedication to its role and social function. Given these factors, is it possible for such a system to genuinely relax? It seems unlikely. This combination creates an always-on mindset, where unending activity becomes the essence of life. If the mind ceases to engage or innovate, its vibrancy dims, rendering life meaningless. Deprive a sixth chakra type of contemplation or academic engagement and they lose their zest for life. Factor in the fifth chakra's dedication to future progress and human intellectual evolution, and the potential for burnout becomes even clearer. Moreover, this framework is sustained by an endless stream of energy. The supportive solar plexus chakra acts as the main source of fuel. Essentially, there's no clear anchor point within this system, leaving no room for a break.

In this blueprint, there's a vital lesson: it's crucial to focus on the human aspects of life—the personal, emotional, and simpler facets of existence. With such a combination, there's a pronounced focus on ideas, visions, and accomplishments, often overshadowing the significance of human connections and seemingly "insignificant" moments, i.e., those lacking depth. This personality seeks meaning or utility, but numerous aspects of life don't serve a particular purpose. Not everything needs analyzing, nor must it align with a grander vision. There's also an evident impatience for obstacles or emotions that hinders their progress. This is precisely why the influence of the sacral chakra type and/or the heart chakra type can offer a soothing balance to such a structure.

These three numbers provided a plethora of insights, and this was just an introductory interpretation! There's so much more to discover, but this section offered a solid foundation. If you're inclined to pursue chakra blueprint interpretation professionally, you have the potential to significantly impact others, as many individuals lack this level of self-awareness and crave such perspective.

Now, let's examine another blueprint to give you a sense of a different chakra configuration.

4–5–7

This blueprint illustrates a primary heart chakra type, followed by a secondary throat chakra and a supportive crown chakra.

When the throat chakra emerges as a secondary chakra type, it often signifies roles like teaching and influencing. However, the combination of the heart and throat chakras deviates significantly from the characteristics of a primary sixth chakra, shared previously. As a result, this blueprint's role isn't confined to disseminating knowledge. Since the heart chakra is the primary chakra type, it defines a distinct way of mentoring.

When the supportive crown chakra is incorporated, it brings an energy governed by water and air elements. The secondary throat chakra type, blending both air and fire, provides a balance to this system, introducing a fiery element. This structure isn't solely about emotions and spirituality; the throat chakra adds a specific direction to it. This guiding force embodies a passionate energy, emphasizing progression, focus, and ambition.

When the heart chakra type combines with the throat chakra type, what insights do they offer to the world? They shed light on emotional growth and mastering relationships. The magic of possessing the throat chakra as a secondary influence is its innate urge to share: wisdom from the primary chakra is naturally voiced and becomes a lesson for others. An individual's emotional evolution transforms into lessons for the broader community. However, this trajectory isn't solely about lofty philosophies. For those rooted in the heart chakra, its true essence becomes clear when viewed as selfless service and dedication to others. The heart chakra transcends the desire for broad influence, personal accolades, or an enchantment with one's own insights. For the heart-centric, the throat chakra's communicative prowess isn't aimed at the multitudes. Instead of impacting the "world" in a generalized sense, they favor more personalized interactions or smaller collectives. Broad, impersonal engagements don't resonate with their core ethos.

However, there's an inherent tension between the fourth and fifth chakra types. Caretakers aren't particularly inclined to influence others or make a significant impression. (This echoes the disposition of the sixth chakra type, which primarily seeks solitude and introspection.) When the heart chakra aligns with the throat chakra, there's an internal struggle: a yearning to impart knowledge but a reluctance to actually do so. Moreover, underlying this dichotomy is the influence of the crown chakra, acting as the supportive type. Its introverted nature further reduces the heart chakra's enthusiasm for outward action.

Central to this soul design is an intrinsic need to guide and inspire others for true fulfillment. Such individuals must wholly merge with this purpose. The nuance here is that those aligned with the heart chakra often gravitate toward one pivotal relationship, overlooking the multitude who could benefit from their influence. Thus, they risk limiting their potential. They must grasp that their journey goes beyond individual aspirations; it's woven into the fabric of their soul.

One must always remember that true joy doesn't stem from the secondary chakra type. While this individual finds completion via the throat chakra, genuine happiness arises from dedication and acts of service. This paves the way for their unique expression. Their guiding mantra often becomes, "Service is my essence. Through love and closeness, I communicate." This sentiment embodies their truest form of connection, one that deeply resonates with them.

When these core beliefs waver, the entire essence of the chakra system is compromised. It's essential for them to always have a driving purpose in their endeavors. Continuously asking "Why this? What's the purpose?" keeps them connected to their heart's intention, igniting their passion and vitality. The heart's zeal is their main energy source. In this unique setup, the crown chakra also energizes them, but its primary role is to amplify expressions emanating from the heart.

One notable aspect of this chakra blueprint is the inherent tension between the fourth and seventh chakra types. The heart chakra type embodies selflessness, often to the point of self-neglect. Such individuals consistently prioritize others, depleting their energy in service. Conversely, the crown chakra type emphasizes self-reflection and spiritual self-care, advocating for personal time dedicated to spiritual growth. For the heart chakra individual, this self-focus can feel unduly selfish, even when it's in the form of the crown chakra's meditative practices. But without such spiritual nourishment, they risk draining their energy reservoirs, pulling from both emotional wells and their physical vitality. This acts as a warning for this chakra combination: there's a genuine risk of self-harm if they don't harness the balancing energies of the crown chakra.

Even this quick summary of the 4–5–7 chakra blueprint clearly illustrates the tensions within the system and how they might be resolved.

Practice
· · · · · · ·
READING YOUR OWN BLUEPRINT

I trust that at this point, you're gaining a deeper understanding of the nuances involved in interpreting chakra blueprints. Now, it's your chance to practice using the nine fundamental questions.

Analyze

Set aside a minimum of thirty minutes to explore your own blueprint using the nine fundamental questions as a guide. Each question is supplemented with several additional questions, designed to deepen your insights and enrich your reflection.

Commit to this process. Be patient. Resist making snap judgments or resorting to hasty, imprecise statements. Aim to uncover as much detail as you can. Remember to enjoy the journey. There's a genuine pleasure in uncovering this hidden world, fueled by your instincts, emotions, and sharpened reading skills.

Naturally, this initial reading might not capture the full essence of your blueprint. However, dedicating thirty minutes to it, even in this early phase, will certainly provide a comprehensive analysis. Once you've completed that half hour, transition to the Declare section for more detailed guidance.

1. **How does the blueprint manifest energetically?** Consider the dominant elements: are they earth, water, fire, or air? Does the

energy lean toward being active or passive, hot or cold, and is it effective or not? Are the elements harmonized, or do the chakras collectively strengthen the energy? Could the energy mix be perceived as serene? Take note of any absent components in the structure.

2. **What emerges when the primary and secondary chakra types combine?** What distinctive tendencies or traits arise from this blend? Delve into strengths and weaknesses. What unique contributions might your blend offer to the world? How can this combination serve or benefit others? Does this combination hint at any careers or roles?

3. **How does the secondary chakra type complement the primary, and conversely, how might it challenge it?** How might the primary and secondary types clash or conflict? Can you identify the range of feelings or states, both positive and negative, that might arise from the chakras' interaction? Does the presence of the supportive chakra amplify any tension between them? What dimension does the supportive chakra introduce to this combination? Are there ways to mitigate this tension by aligning more with the primary type?

4. **What stands out as the benefits and remarkable attributes of this specific blueprint?**

5. **Which aspects of this constellation need to be acknowledged and embraced as unchangeable?**

6. **What are the potential risks or self-sabotaging tendencies inherent in this structure?** Where could this structure pose a major imbalance?

7. **What wisdom does this pattern offer?** What life lessons can be gleaned from this blueprint?

8. **How can the full potential of this blueprint be harnessed?** In your current life—from work to relationships to the challenges you're facing—what innate strengths can you lean on?

9. **How can the interplay between the primary and secondary elements be stabilized?** How can you achieve harmony

through your social connections, surroundings, pursuits, and inner work? Focus on reconciling the primary and secondary connections and finding equilibrium within the entire structure. Keep in mind that understanding the four "overlooked" chakra types can offer profound insight into cultivating balance.

Declare

10. Dedicate fifteen minutes to crafting your soul's mission statement based on your analysis. A mission statement puts your introspections into a definitive declaration. This isn't about showcasing anything to the world. Rather, aim to answer profound questions, such as: *Who am I? Why am I here? How do I plan to achieve my purpose? What strengths can I harness? What are my unique gifts, and how do I envision utilizing these gifts?*

    You needn't approach this methodically. However, transforming your self-reflection into a personal proclamation heightens your awareness and underscores the significance of your blueprint—or at least a facet of it. Let your declaration be along the lines of: "I am these three chakra types. This is my nature, these are my passions, and this is what my heart desires. This is why I am here, and here's how I plan to achieve it. These are my talents," and so on.

11. Examine whether the statement you wrote resonates with your core self. Reading it should feel like a mirror is reflecting the dynamic forces within you. While it may encapsulate your essence, it's also a beacon, hinting at your untapped potential.

Practice
• • • • • •
READING SOMEONE ELSE'S BLUEPRINT

There are three approaches to interpreting another's blueprint:

- Test your interpretative skills by generating three random numbers. Explore the possible personality traits that would arise from this triad.
- Investigate the blueprint of someone you know intimately by guessing their three-chakra alignment as you perceive it.
- Involve a friend who's open to the experience. Engage in a lively conversation as you analyze their blueprint using the nine fundamental questions. Explain that you're in the initial stages of mastering this technique, ensuring they understand it's a practice run. Remember, you're not expected to have perfected the method just yet. Your aim is to familiarize yourself with analyzing a tangible personality and discerning an underlying pattern based on chakra alignment. Relish the moments when your friend validates your insight, and be open to their counterpoints or differing perspectives. Engage in a two-way discussion, making this a collaborative journey of discovery.

Regardless of your chosen method, allocate a minimum of thirty minutes for a detailed and insightful reading. Approach the exercise with an open mind and a lighthearted spirit.

SEVEN

A GLIMPSE INTO THE FORTY-TWO CHAKRA COMBINATIONS

By now, you've cultivated a foundational understanding of the dynamics of each chakra within the three-tiered system: their individual functions, interrelations, and the equilibrium, influences, and challenges they introduce. This chapter explores the forty-two possible primary and secondary combinations, which create distinct personality types. Though this look at each type will be succinct, these snapshots will enrich your understanding of the integration between primary and secondary chakra types. Additionally, these characterizations might pave the way for a clearer, more grounded understanding of your own chakra blueprint.

Consider the forty-two personality types as products of a unique marriage: a union between the primary chakra type and its secondary counterpart. Like any marriage, this union can flourish with joy and harmony, but it's not exempt from challenges. While some marriages find their rhythm effortlessly, others demand dedication and effort. Regardless of the journey, this union births a distinct personality that embodies the virtues and challenges of both chakras.

This emerging personality stands in stark contrast to the singular chakra type that one might imagine. As you explore the descriptions, the path charted by each chakra pairing becomes evident. The contrasts can be striking. For instance, a person with a root chakra paired with a sacral chakra will behave very differently than someone whose root chakra is paired with a solar plexus chakra. Remember, if you seek a deeper comprehension of yourself, your life's journey, your path to fulfillment, and your inner balance, you must look at more than your primary chakra type. It has become evident that in primary-secondary chakra combinations, one type shapes your life experiences, purpose, and joy. In contrast, the other directs your path, instilling in you specific tendencies that guide your actions and pursuits. Look at it this way: the primary type represents your face, while the secondary type determines where your gaze is directed.

Root Chakra Combinations

You're about to delve into combinations that have the root chakra as the primary chakra type. For those attuned to the root chakra type, this is your chance to discern which of the six pairings you feel most connected to.

1–2

The harmonious blend of the root chakra and the sacral chakra serves as an exemplary representation of balance and unity. Combining the sacral chakra with the root chakra results in a more vibrant and effervescent root energy, akin to the earth being rejuvenated by water. This duo revel in their mutual appreciation for sensory experiences, the physical realm, and a tangible connection to the earth.

While the root chakra offers stability, the sacral chakra encourages a life that joyfully acknowledges the earth's bounty. This unique synergy is evident in their bond with nature. These individuals are deeply connected to the land, perhaps through agricultural endeavors. They are driven by an innate love for nature rather than simply respecting its order.

Moreover, this combination can foster personalities that, while grounded and diligent, are drawn to vibrant expressions of life, such as dance, humor, and adventure, thereby diluting the conventional boundaries of the root chakra. However, a paradox exists: while the root chakra emphasizes structure and commitment, the sacral thrives on change and occasionally challenges established norms. Balancing these dynamics necessitates a firm foundation in the root chakra's core principles.

1–3

When the root chakra type is combined with a secondary solar plexus chakra type, a dynamic, potent energy emerges, amplifying the fiery essence of the root chakra. This pairing is characterized by diligence, intensity, discipline, and structure. The steady and deliberate energy of the root chakra undergoes a transformation, resulting in enhanced capabilities for construction and steadfastness. However, this isn't just about systematic building, as is typical of the root chakra. Instead, it's about building with visionary goals in mind.

Both chakras share a mutual dedication to perseverance and tenacity. In this union, the attributes of persistence and efficiency are amplified. Aspirations align with the root chakra's passion for establishing order, fostering harmony, and enhancing systems. Consequently, there's a relentless drive toward growth.

This combination offers considerable benefits, as the root chakra stabilizes the solar plexus chakra by anchoring it to structures, frameworks, familial ties, and routines. It's essential for these individuals to remain mindful of becoming overly consumed by ambition. Their aspirations exist primarily to promote harmony and support the structures of life.

1–4

Combining the root chakra type and the heart chakra type yields one of the most harmonious pairings imaginable, a beautifully balanced and calming blend. This union gives rise to a genuinely benevolent, relaxed, and warm-hearted individual, with the heart chakra infusing an added touch of sweetness. These two types deeply value peace, harmony, and the comforting presence of family. Such a union is characteristic of a community-loving, family-centric disposition. Those with this combination go beyond craving safety and security—they have a deep-seated desire for emotional connectivity.

These individuals thrive on cultivating harmonious familial and community bonds. They are always aiming to uplift and serve the collective. Their character is devoted, loyal, accountable, and tranquil, and this combination is not typically driven by high-flying ambitions. There is no pressing need to adhere strictly to the root chakra's values, so a sense of unity remains consistent.

1–5

In individuals with a secondary throat chakra, there's a distinct interest in education and instruction. They are propelled to share their knowledge about their passions, leading to teaching as a form of fulfillment. The essence of this blend is to empower others with fundamental tools to enhance their lives. These individuals guide others toward harmony and balance in various aspects, be it in their physical health, familial relationships, community, technological proficiency, conservation efforts, or time management.

This combination has a unique perspective that extends beyond the typical limits of the root chakra. The throat chakra can induce tension, particularly when combined with introverted traits. While the throat chakra gravitates toward influencing others and having a public role, the root chakra cherishes humility and discretion. It's crucial for these individuals to uphold their intrinsic values while remaining devoted to enlightening others, avoiding the urge to withhold knowledge.

1–6

In this combination, the nuances of the third eye chakra blend with the foundational traits of the root chakra, creating a light and airy spirit. This is linked to the third eye chakra's passion for intellectual endeavors and exploration. This blend creates a dynamic, active energy, and these individuals would make exceptional scientists. They are methodical and attentive to detail, and they harness unparalleled creativity. These individuals are drawn to subjects such as balance, health, and the law, perhaps even the mysteries of universal and divine laws.

The combined force of these chakras results in a desire for disciplined living. It's almost fanatical, given that both chakras yearn for a tranquil, orchestrated life. Yet a tension is palpable, as the third eye chakra attempts to shift the root chakra toward abstract thinking. It's vital, then, to remain anchored in the essence of the root chakra; all intellectual quests should uphold and resonate with its intrinsic values.

1–7

The combining of the root chakra and the crown chakra is truly remarkable, as it brings together opposite ends of the chakra system. This blend embodies the union of the tangible physical realm and the ethereal spiritual realm. Essentially, it's as if heaven and earth converged in a life steeped in spirituality, tradition, and the intertwining of law and spirit. Such a personality strives to anchor their spiritual essence in the earthly realm while elevating the tangible world closer to the spiritual plane. Though these individuals are grounded, they do not have an overpowering attachment to the material world.

The density of the root chakra is counterbalanced by the loftiness of the crown chakra. The duality within this personality is apparent, generating tension due to its contrasting nature. To alleviate this tension, it's essential to lead a life anchored in religious and traditional principles. Things should be structured, allowing the core values of the root chakra to be fully honored.

Sacral Chakra Combinations

Now, let's enter the domain of the sacral chakra. Those who identify with the primary sacral chakra type, pay close attention; you might discover a description that resonates deeply with you.

2–1

Blending a primary sacral chakra and a secondary root chakra leads to an individual with a sense of balance and a strong connection to reality. The root chakra's grounding influence encourages stability, harmony, community, familial ties, and potentially more consistent creative expression. This pairing effectively counters many of the sacral chakra's pitfalls, including a tendency to procrastinate, a lack of commitment, and self-destructive habits. In this combination, the sacral chakra continues to pursue a vivid life, enriched with deep emotions and physical experiences, but it's oriented toward a structured existence that many Artists might otherwise avoid.

However, this union also has its challenges. These individuals must ensure that they maintain their vibrant energy so that discipline doesn't dampen their spirit. Ultimately, it's vital to acknowledge that a structured lifestyle is designed to amplify the sacral chakra's fiery energy, and this core motivation should always be remembered.

2–3

When the sacral chakra and the solar plexus chakra types combine, there is an electrifying surge of energy. This dynamic pairing is commonly found in professional athletes, as it offers an abundance of physical prowess, thrill-seeking tendencies, and relentless vitality. At the same time, it's coupled with a driving ambition, a competitive edge, and a thirst for challenge. These individuals radiate energy, passion, and impulsiveness, and they often struggle to direct this overwhelming power. They might veer toward self-destructive behaviors simply because channeling such intense energy proves difficult. Their emotional landscape can be turbulent, marked by mood swings and occasional instability.

A unique tension arises between these chakras. The dominant sacral chakra seeks spontaneous enjoyment and pleasure, whereas the solar plexus chakra strives for achievement and triumph. Since the solar plexus chakra isn't the primary force here, it's essential to harness its vigor without letting it overshadow the playful essence of the sacral chakra type. These individuals might sometimes feel overwhelmed by the relentless competitive grind, particularly if they're surrounded by solar plexus–dominated individuals who are solely fixated on success. Consider athletes as an illustration; some might yearn to engage in sports primarily for fun rather than victory. While this chakra combination isn't exclusive to athletes, they serve as a clear example.

2–4

Combining the sacral chakra type and the heart chakra type yields a personality that is ethereal, deeply emotional, and sensuous. These chakras temper each other, resulting in an uncompetitive nature. These individuals connect with the world through rich experiences and personal interactions. Their journey toward fulfillment is characterized by deep emotional bonds, often sought in pursuit of their perfect match. Their life is largely dictated by emotional ties, which influence decisions ranging from their career path to their personal lifestyle choices. A lack of ambition means these individuals often lean on others to provide direction, even though their sacral chakra might push them to occasionally resist external guidance.

These individuals truly flourish in a nurturing and affectionate setting, be it a relationship, a friendship, or even a supportive workplace. They thrive when they're accepted *and* guided, because if they are left on their own, they might struggle to chart their own course.

2–5

When the sacral chakra merges with the throat chakra, a sacral mentor is born. Such mentors hold significant roles in society, often emerging as instructors in tantra, conscious movement, bodywork, or yoga. Some might even pioneer innovative techniques or healing practices. Their depth of experience allows them to lead transformative groups or guide shamanic explorations. In other spheres, they shine as copywriters or coaches, brimming with creative insights rooted in visual and sensual domains. Interestingly, this combination is commonly found in comedians and musicians, emphasizing their natural ability to articulate the sacral experience. When people with this pairing work as educators or influencers, their zest, wit, and vivacity make their messages infectious.

However, a unique conflict exists between the sacral and throat chakras. While these individuals are bursting with enthusiasm, they may be inconsistent when it comes to ambition or a sustained vision for the future. This can lead to periods of fluctuating commitment, making them appear dishonest or unreliable at times.

2–6

When a primary sacral chakra type combines with a secondary third eye chakra, the outcome is intriguing. This union results in an ethereal, abstract blend of emotions and thoughts. Essentially, it creates a sacral chakra explorer, an individual who dives into life experiences that resonate with this archetype. Investigations might revolve around sensuality, vitality, desire, passion, the natural world, animals, or kinetic expressions. Imagine someone who carefully interacts with animals while meticulously documenting their behaviors. This dynamic creates individuals who feel intensely and yet possess a somewhat-detached perspective. However, their learning approach isn't merely intellectual or systematic—it's charged with fervor. The driving force for these individuals is enthusiasm; they are drawn to subjects that truly ignite their passion.

A dichotomy exists between these two chakra energies. While the third eye chakra embodies objectivity, a scientific mindset, and logical reasoning, the sacral chakra thrives on raw emotion and stays within the experiential realm. It's vital to ensure that any scholarly pursuits enhance life's experiences rather than diminishing or overshadowing them.

2–7

Merging the sacral chakra and the crown chakra yields an ethereal blend, perhaps even more so than with the heart or third eye chakras. This union manifests a harmonious rhythm, with both types immersing themselves in the present moment, valuing the experience over any tangible gains.

However, this free-flowing nature can also pose challenges, as it lacks the conventional drive or functional capabilities found in other combinations. Often, these individuals gravitate toward spiritual environments, like ashrams or spiritual communities. These settings provide the freedom necessary for this metaphorical butterfly to flit about unburdened. Moreover, the sacral chakra type has profound spiritual potential, as Artists fully devote themselves to experiences.

This unique coupling can result in individuals of profound spiritual depth, but tension remains. While the crown chakra leans toward transcendence or life's dissolution, the sacral chakra revels in the sensory joys of existence. Balancing these contrasting desires can be a challenge.

Solar Plexus Chakra Combinations

Now, shift your attention to the domain of the solar plexus chakra. If you resonate with the primary solar plexus type, closely read the upcoming descriptions. You might discover a reflection of yourself.

3–1

What occurs when the solar plexus chakra combines with the root chakra? This fusion of the solar plexus and root chakras culminates in an assertive structure, characterized by endurance and long-term planning and projects. Unlike the 1–3 chakra combination, a primary solar plexus chakra doesn't propel the root chakra forward. Instead, the secondary root chakra stabilizes the solar plexus chakra. The result is a balanced blend that mitigates many of the challenges inherent to the solar plexus type. This creates community-oriented individuals, driven to establish or maintain structures that foster cohesion and stability. While the ambition of the solar plexus chakra remains undiminished, its aims shift toward building entities like organizations, foundations, and online platforms.

There's inherent tension due to the root chakra countering the dramatic tendencies of the solar plexus chakra. The goal isn't to evolve into a traditional Builder, but to channel the Achiever's ambition in a more focused manner.

3–2

When the solar plexus chakra combines with the sacral chakra, it is an erratic and unsteady combination. Given that the solar plexus is energized by the sacral chakra and not vice versa, these individuals brim with energy but are unsure of its direction. They align their vigor with the free-spirited, explosive essence of the sacral chakra.

However, there's an inherent friction between the second and third chakra personalities: the sacral chakra's nature dampens the drive of the solar plexus chakra, much like extinguishing a flame with water. Hence, it's crucial to understand how to channel and realize ambitions within the solar plexus chakra's domain.

While these individuals remain predominantly solar plexus–centric, goals should be steered toward the sacral realm. Navigating this energy constructively is essential, as there's a risk of veering toward addiction, hedonism, and excess.

3–4

This pairing is unique and perhaps seldom encountered. Merging the solar plexus chakra with the heart chakra creates a captivating dynamic, as the heart chakra profoundly influences the direction of the solar plexus chakra. The heart chakra acts like a soothing balm, calming the intense nature of the solar plexus chakra. While the essence of the solar plexus chakra remains, its objectives and aspirations become intertwined with the heart's focus on relationships, community service, and even selflessness. This combination brings to mind those who make significant sacrifices for their nation or a cherished cause.

This union is not without its challenges. While the heart chakra mitigates some of the solar plexus's pitfalls (such as egoism, a lack of empathy, and notable tendencies toward anger), it can also hinder its ambitious pursuits. This scenario underscores the importance of staying true to one's primary nature. By doing so, individuals with this combination can achieve remarkable, selfless feats for the greater good.

3–5

When the solar plexus chakra combines with the throat chakra, the result is a potent mentor who specializes in areas of motivation, discipline, self-worth, and achievement. But this fusion offers more depth than one might initially perceive. When combined, these chakras fuel a powerful forward momentum. These individuals are marked by their lofty ambitions, which aren't just about personal gain. They aim to pioneer change and transform the future.

This pairing also has its extremes. There's an intensity—a fiery passion—which, if unchecked, can manifest as overbearing or confrontational behaviors. Both chakras amplify each other's aspirations, emphasizing immense possibility and potential. However, their combined vigor can sometimes overshadow empathy and lead them to disregard the challenges or feelings of others. Intriguingly, the synergy of these chakras can sometimes be the very thing they must overcome.

3–6

When the solar plexus chakra combines with the third eye chakra, individuals passionately research or study matters of the solar plexus. They are driven to understand success, analyzing factors like personal achievements, the rise of billionaires, or the methods behind prosperous startups. This combination exudes a fiery energy, intensified by the intellectual fervor of the mind.

However, there's an inherent tension. The third eye chakra gravitates toward abstract thought, while the solar plexus chakra prefers worldly control. This dichotomy can be addressed by channeling abstract ideas into the realm of the solar plexus and seeing the act of research as a fulfilling ambition. While the third eye chakra promotes introspection and detachment, the solar plexus chakra seeks dominance in the real world. In this dynamic, the solar plexus takes precedence, and these individuals use intellectual insight as a means to an end.

3–7

When the solar plexus chakra is complemented by the crown chakra, individuals are a unique blend of the tangible and ethereal. The crown chakra, with its airy and elevating essence, offers the solar plexus chakra an intriguing spiritual redirection. Traditionally, the solar plexus chakra centers on material mastery and triumph in the physical world. When merged with the crown chakra, this drive pivots toward the spiritual realm. Visualize a yogi or a shaman rooted in the solar plexus chakra but guided by spiritual ambition; their quests would revolve around acquiring spiritual power, uncovering arcane wisdom, or even pursuing the allure of enlightenment—a lofty goal that, to the solar plexus chakra, seems like the pinnacle of achievement.

However, the inherent tranquility of the seventh chakra, which seeks a state of pure stillness, does conflict with the fiery ambitions of the solar plexus chakra. Tension isn't about extinguishing the fire within, but rather channeling its warmth in a new, transformative direction.

Heart Chakra Combinations

Let's get to know the combinations of the heart chakra. If you resonate with the primary heart chakra type, pay close attention to these blends. Do any reflect your essence?

4–1

The root chakra and heart chakra, when combined, create a harmonious and balanced connection, and in this context, the heart chakra dominates. The emphasis is on relationships, serving others, the broader struggles of humanity, and loved ones. When the heart chakra is paired with the root chakra, there's a compelling drive to build a solid foundation—or maybe even build a shelter—to ensure a stable environment for all. These individuals have an inherent desire to cater to others' needs, all the while embodying genuine love and care. The alignment between the chakras is harmonious and complementary; this blend results in individuals who are emotionally rich but also pragmatic and hardworking. Their devotion isn't mere sentiment—it demands real action to achieve genuine fulfillment.

4–2

When the heart chakra combines with a secondary sacral chakra, an intriguing dynamic emerges. This combination feels distinctly passive, largely due to the sacral chakra's flowing nature. Such a configuration leads to an emotional archetype that embodies fluidity. The heart chakra's intense dedication to others undergoes a transformation in this union, resulting in a more open and transient love. This might manifest as short-lived yet deeply meaningful moments with others.

It's easy to recognize the underlying tension between these chakras. The heart chakra represents commitment, loyalty, and connections with others, while the sacral chakra leans toward self-sufficiency and avoids anything binding. This blend results in a unique emotional state, evident in specific moments or phases, that offers a refreshing perspective on the nature of love.

4–3

In this pairing, the heart and solar plexus chakras combine. This union feels more fluid and organic than its inverse counterpart; it acts as a catalyst, invigorating the heart chakra and igniting a passionate flame within. With the solar plexus chakra playing a secondary role to the heart chakra, there's a heightened sense of purpose and direction. Emotion, compassion, and the desire to make a difference are now channeled into ambitious pursuits. When allowed to flourish, these individuals can be transformative on a global scale, representing an archetype that harnesses love's power in assertive and actionable ways.

Inherent contradictions exist. While the heart chakra yearns for intimate connections and shies away from grand ambition, the solar plexus chakra exudes a revolutionary zest. These complexities can be navigated smoothly as long as the heart chakra remains the guiding force.

4–5

When a primary heart chakra type combines with a secondary throat chakra type, it creates a harmonious blend that ignites the heart with passion, albeit not as intensely as in the previous pairing. These individuals often take on a mentorship role, guiding others in matters of emotion, personal growth, and relationships. Their experiences become lessons meant to be shared to help others navigate similar journeys. This chakra pairing often shoulders the responsibility of paving the way for others via their own challenges and obstacles. It's essential for them to embrace their guiding role, even when the heart chakra's instinct might be for them to close themselves off.

This combination embodies a vision, suggesting that their purpose is not just about emotional connection. These individuals must also realize their grander ambitions, like fostering a more compassionate society or pursuing the kind of love that reshapes the world. This lends them a profound sense of idealism.

4–6

The heart chakra and the third eye chakra are a fascinating blend, offering an airy mix of emotion and thought. This combination strikes a harmonious balance between sentiment and wisdom. At its core, these individuals are characterized by emotional intensity. Alongside emotion, there's a compelling desire to delve into the subject of their focus. Imagine feeling a profound love for a revered figure and then being driven to explore the teachings of that individual, for example. There's an immense emotional depth, but it's coupled with an intellectual curiosity that seeks to articulate feelings as refined concepts.

Given that the third eye chakra guides fulfillment for these individuals, true understanding and contentment only come when emotions are also intellectually grasped. This presents a potential challenge: while the heart chakra yearns for raw, unfiltered emotional experiences, the third eye chakra can sometimes create a barrier, potentially distancing them from the very emotions they are trying to understand. The resolution? Always begin with the heart.

4–7

The fusion of a primary heart chakra and a secondary crown chakra creates an ethereal structure, best understood as a profound love for the divine or a dedication to spiritual pursuits. Here, the heart chakra's desires are only truly met through spiritual endeavors. These individuals might resonate with Bhakti yoga, centered on love and unwavering devotion. They see everything through the lens of their singular, ultimate devotion. Their approach is straightforward and pure, driven by their specific focus on their object of veneration. Typically, these individuals flourish in spiritual environments, be it under the guidance of a spiritual teacher, in an ashram, or in a monastery.

While brimming with heartfelt energy, these individuals may be drawn to solitude, silence, and introspection, especially if the seventh chakra were to dominate. But here, the heart chakra is in charge, leading these individuals to serve humanity in honor of their devotion. This combination is the embodiment of unwavering dedication and devotion.

Throat Chakra Combinations

The following chakras are the three most ethereal: the throat, third eye, and crown. Let's explore the throat chakra's interactions when paired with the six secondary types.

5–1

This union creates a predominantly active energy, intensifying the throat chakra's fiery emphasis on vision, leadership, and the realization of aspirations. However, the grounding nature of the root chakra stabilizes the throat chakra, counteracting its tendency toward dreaminess. While the throat chakra is often associated with the fire element, it also has airy qualities that sometimes overshadow practical details. In this pairing, the throat chakra dreams expansively and exerts wide-reaching influence, whereas the root chakra translates these ambitions into persistent, long-term actions.

This synergy isn't without its contradictions. The root chakra's focus on details and steady progression can sometimes dampen the fervent passion of the throat chakra. It's crucial to recognize that the root chakra primarily acts as a means to achieve these dreams. As a secondary chakra, it empowers the throat chakra to manifest its envisioned changes, be they in structure, institution, or organization, which makes this a potent combination.

5–2

Combining the throat chakra and the sacral chakra leads to a passive energy. The sacral chakra has a cooling, airy influence on the throat chakra, which already possesses an airy nature. The resulting energy is like a sporadic burst—energy expresses itself in fleeting, influential moments rather than in a sustained, consistent direction. A tension emerges between the momentary, immediate focus of the sacral chakra and the forward-thinking, visionary aspirations of the throat chakra. This dynamic may lead these individuals to grapple with inherent frustrations.

The challenge here is for individuals to ground themselves in the throat chakra while harnessing the sacral chakra's spontaneity for innovative, unexpected, and creative manifestations. This blend (and its inverse counterpart, 2–5) is especially well-suited for artists. With the sacral chakra in the primary role, energy is naturally channeled toward expressive endeavors, making this a smooth fusion.

5–3

When the throat chakra type combines with the solar plexus chakra type, the result is a potent, active energy, amplifying the fiery essence of the throat chakra. The solar plexus chakra propels all ambitions toward actualization with unparalleled vigor. The synergy of the fifth and third chakras is powerfully intense, especially with the throat chakra at the helm, channeling the solar plexus chakra's relentless drive to bring dreams to life. These individuals are charismatic and adept at influencing, inspiring, and strategizing. They might naturally take on leadership roles, guiding organizations, driving pivotal projects, or creating companies. These individuals excel at forward movement, shaping the future with the throat chakra's idealism and the solar plexus chakra's drive. The throat chakra's usual challenge of putting ideas into action is neutralized here.

This combination may create an intense personality that, given its focus, occasionally overlooks emotions, interpersonal nuances, and relationships. Being close to such an individual could be a demanding experience.

5–4

When the throat chakra combines with the heart chakra, there is a harmonizing and delicate synergy. This union beautifully addresses the throat chakra's difficulty connecting with others. Often, the throat chakra is consumed by its own ideas, visions, and paradigms, sidelining the sentiments of others. However, in this pairing, the emphasis shifts to relationship-building, communication, intimacy, and service. This means that the throat chakra's aspirations are seamlessly converted into heartfelt connections, serving as the primary avenue of influence and articulation—a truly captivating manifestation. Both chakras belong to the emotional-communicative category, which ensures that their collaboration is fluid.

However, the heart chakra's nurturing nature can temper the throat chakra's ambition, causing potential friction. The heart chakra seeks emotional depth and closeness, while the throat chakra aims for visionary leadership. Despite this tension, it's essential to recognize that the secondary heart chakra is a vessel, aiding the fulfillment of the throat chakra's objectives.

5–6

When a primary throat chakra and a secondary third eye chakra combine, a cooling and relatively soothing synergy emerges. Though both chakras possess elements of fire, their union tends to amplify their airy characteristics. This is largely because the fiery essence is dependent on external influences.

This union presents an innate dichotomy. The throat chakra's fervor for expression and influence becomes muted by the third eye chakra's preference for introspection, observation, and research. This might cause these individuals to swing between a strong urge to express their thoughts and a desire for quiet reflection, which is typical of the third eye chakra. One way to harmonize this tension is to lean into roles like that of a researcher, educator, or expert, particularly in areas related to vision and conceptualization.

The harmony of this alignment often depends on the attributes introduced by the supportive chakra. Though the throat chakra possesses the potential for self-fulfillment, it may struggle to express its essence externally. These individuals might wrestle with powerful impulses, only to be subsequently drawn into the reflectiveness of the third eye chakra. Resolution lies in anchoring themselves firmly in the throat chakra's domain and recognizing the third eye chakra's role, which is merely to offer depth to their visions and passions. When properly aligned, this combination has the potential to birth innovative and groundbreaking ideas, leveraging the third eye chakra's unconventional insights.

5–7

The combination of the throat and crown chakras exudes a serene, soft energy. Merging these two chakras typically gives rise to a potent force, often manifesting as an inspiring guide capable of conveying deep spiritual truths in a transformative manner. However, this synergy is most profound when led by the crown chakra—such an arrangement signifies teachings stemming from deep spiritual roots, later articulated through the throat chakra. When the fifth chakra takes precedence, the drive for expression predominantly channels itself through spiritual domains, thus defining its mode of fulfillment.

This dynamic isn't simple. The throat chakra's inherent drive to articulate becomes so spiritually inclined that it almost counters itself, presenting an internal paradox. The remedy lies in anchoring firmly in the primary chakra, as is often the case. The crown chakra should be recognized as a conduit for deeper spiritual fulfillment.

A notable benefit of this combination is its ability to temper the dominating tendencies of the throat chakra, promoting balance and harmony.

Third Eye Chakra Combinations

Enter the realm of the third eye chakra. If you resonate with a primary third eye chakra type, read closely. You might recognize yourself in one of the upcoming descriptions.

6–1

When the third eye chakra combines with the root chakra, an active synergy emerges, amplifying the fiery element of both chakras. Although the root chakra naturally lacks fire, its presence is heightened in this combination. However, the magic of this union lies in its grounding quality. It moves the intellectual and theoretical tendencies of the sixth chakra toward tangible, earthly outcomes. Such a blend greatly diminishes the inherent conflicts of the third eye chakra, which often resists physical experiences and everyday life.

This pairing is not without its contradictions, though. While the root chakra leans toward practicality, the third eye chakra is drawn to contemplation and abstraction. By embracing the essence of the third eye, every idea seeks and finds a concrete form, suggesting that from this combination's perspective, ideas lose significance if they remain unmanifested. These individuals often manifest as balanced scholars, likely engrossed in understanding the innate order of things. However, this combination also fosters a penchant for routine and predictability. In any given blend, the third eye and root chakras yearn for repetition, consistent patterns, and unwavering control, adding an intriguing layer to this dynamic.

6–2

The melding of the third eye chakra and the sacral chakra produces a gentle, ethereal, and soothing energy. The third eye chakra thrives in contemplation, while the sacral chakra is anchored to tangible experiences. This synergy creates a profound internal universe. With such emotional richness, this union could inspire artists, perhaps poets or painters. However, while captivating, this mix isn't necessarily pragmatic, as these individuals may not have the practical means for real-world accomplishment. The supportive chakra plays a pivotal role for these individuals.

A natural tension exists: the sacral chakra gravitates toward tangible sensations, contrasting the third eye chakra's interest in intellectual reflection. Yet this union allows the third eye chakra's musings to manifest as tangible experiences, defying the inherent tendency to merely observe. Instead, these individuals actively engage with life.

6–3

Combining the third eye chakra and the solar plexus chakra results in a potent, dynamic, and assertive individual. The solar plexus chakra amplifies the third eye chakra's fiery attributes. This union creates individuals who are fulfilled through ambition; perhaps they have a drive for unparalleled excellence. Think of a distinguished researcher, someone thriving on recognition and continually aiming to be the best in their field.

For this combination, research and study aren't merely intellectual pursuits. True satisfaction comes from a sense of competition and achieving notable success. Visualize a scholar or an inventor propelled to make their mark. The journey isn't solely about gaining knowledge—it's about the accolades that accompany significant breakthroughs.

A tension exists. The solar plexus chakra seeks worldly accolades, while the third eye chakra might see such pursuits as superficial. Nonetheless, this union can be highly productive, provided that the third eye chakra's love of learning remains uninhibited.

6–4

When the third eye chakra combines with the heart chakra, a light and gentle blend emerges. This is largely due to the heart chakra enhancing the third eye chakra's airy qualities.

It is worth noting that this union doesn't necessarily pave the way for tangible achievement or clarity in the material realm. The third eye chakra represents depth, curiosity, and the quest for knowledge, whereas the heart chakra pursues emotional wholeness and fulfillment. This synthesis means that intellectual endeavors must intertwine with emotional connections and relationships, which can create a beautiful dynamic. Such a pairing steers the typically introspective third eye chakra toward warmth and empathy, making it more relationally attuned.

While it's crucial to retain the inherent values and purpose of the third eye chakra, the wisdom garnered should be generously shared. Instead of adopting the throat chakra's assertive manner, these individuals should focus on selfless service, unwavering devotion, and intimate bonds. Rather than a scholar engrossed in solitary study, picture one who actively participating in groups, sharing insights and reveling in mutual discovery, all with a heartfelt touch.

6–5

When the third eye chakra combines with the throat chakra, a dynamic, active fusion occurs. Both chakras amplify each other's fire and air elements, enriching ideas, visions, and dreams. The result? An archetype that's deeply idealistic, almost ethereal, floating in the vast expanse of thoughts and aspirations.

Primarily, this union gives rise to the quintessential educator: one who not only delves into research but is driven to share their knowledge with others. These individuals are in a perpetual state of learning and teaching, with a singular goal: to inspire and enlighten. Even as they absorb new information, they're already conceptualizing ways to translate it into tangible insight, be it in a book or through a course. However, an inherent tension exists: the throat chakra urges engagement with the outside world, whereas the third eye chakra is content with solitary introspection.

6–7

When the inquisitive nature of the third eye chakra meets the transcendent nature of the crown chakra, an intriguing combination arises. This is a deeply passive, airy union. Here, the seventh chakra amplifies the ethereal qualities of the sixth.

In this blend, every intellectual pursuit inevitably veers toward the spiritual, culminating in a state of meditative silence or higher transcendence. This union creates an exceptionally sharp mind, yet one that can't dwell too deeply on philosophy. Thoughts, no matter how profound, tend to evaporate into the vast expanse of the crown chakra. Essentially, the true satisfaction of such a mind is rooted in spiritual exploration and enlightenment. This archetype can be incredibly inspiring; however, these individuals may seem ephemeral, aloof, and even otherworldly, as if they are in a different dimension.

A tension exists: the crown chakra leans toward a state of nonthought, while the third eye chakra is driven by curiosity and analysis. Thus, it's crucial to remain grounded in the third eye chakra and to channel all acquired knowledge through the lens of spiritual existence.

Crown Chakra Combinations

This section concludes the exploration of the forty-two primary and secondary combinations. Crown chakra personalities are undoubtedly the most ethereal. If you resonate with the primary crown chakra type, pay close attention—you might recognize yourself in one of these six combinations.

7–1

When the crown chakra is combined with the root chakra, this powerfully anchors the crown, implying that spiritual endeavors need a structured, harmonious manifestation in the earthly realm. In this union, the crown chakra is compelled to move from its elevated seclusion, seeking purpose in life's modest acts and pragmatic pursuits. This combination conjures images of a saint connected with the earth or a monk who, after a deep spiritual immersion, joyfully tidies the monastery. Such an alignment might also spark an affinity for communal living or an allegiance to time-honored traditions, echoing the root chakra's essence of collective unity.

The tension between the chakras is palpable, as each pull in starkly different directions. Yet with a foundation in the crown chakra, harmony prevails.

7–2

When the crown chakra joins with the sacral chakra, what emerges is a fusion that's both ethereal and unanchored. Defined by a state of pure being and experience, these individuals neither seek worldly achievements nor possess the means to attain them, yet their beauty remains undeniable. Consider a Yogi lost in nature's embrace during meditation, or one whose spirit dances with joy, maybe even with a hint of wild abandon.

Such an individual might eschew conventional work, gravitating instead toward a nomadic lifestyle. Their existence—bursting with sensuality, physicality, and fervor—seems to diverge from traditional spiritual paths. Yet, when these individuals anchor in the crown chakra, the sacral chakra harmoniously aligns with the spirit, finding serenity in this alignment.

7–3

Consider a celestial blend where the crown chakra is infused with the traits of the solar plexus chakra type, the Achiever. Within the context of the crown chakra, this blend introduces a stabilizing, active touch, instilling an unexpected, fiery dynamism. This particular union leads to individuals with a thirst for excellence in spiritual endeavors. Such aspirations aren't tethered to materialistic pursuits but aim to scale peaks of enlightenment, transcendence, meditation, and spiritual mastery. This potent dynamic lends purpose to the typically passive crown chakra.

The inherent dichotomy is evident: while the crown chakra tends to dissolve ambitions, favoring a state of pure existence, the solar plexus chakra leans toward triumph and conquest. However, when aligned, this pairing can function seamlessly. It's vital for these individuals to remain anchored in their spiritual path rather than swaying toward the values solely associated with the solar plexus chakra. In this blend, the solar plexus chakra's vigor uplifts the crown chakra.

7–4

What occurs when the introspective Yogi aligns with the compassionate heart chakra type, termed the Caretaker? This combination forms nurturing and calming individuals, deeply rooted in emotional and spiritual dedication. While there's a comparable synergy between the fourth and seventh chakra types, in this blend, the seventh chakra is pivotal. This means that spiritual pursuits will manifest in an emotional outpouring, linking the individual's spiritual domain to their connections with others. What's captivating about this union is that the typically abstract nature of the crown chakra is drawn into tangible emotional connection, bridging the gap between self and other. These individuals would thrive within a spiritual community, as expressing themselves outside of this context might be challenging.

While the combination of the crown and heart chakras lacks conventional expressive tools, the inherent tension within is minimal. If one were to pinpoint a potential conflict, it might be the contrast of the heart chakra's emotional currents with the detached essence of the crown chakra. However, when anchored in the crown chakra, heart energy emanates naturally from a place of liberation and grace.

7–5

When a primary crown chakra type merges with a secondary throat chakra type, the fusion is fairly evident in its characteristics. This blend is ethereal and lacks a solid foundation, due to the airy essence of the crown chakra. These individuals have plenty of ideas and a compelling need to articulate them, both stemming from the spiritual core of the crown chakra. One benefit is the fiery dynamism of the throat chakra, which channels inspiration and influence. This combination likely manifests as an insightful spiritual guide, capable of igniting others' fervor for spiritual growth.

However, an inherent tension exists. The throat chakra's drive for influence contrasts sharply with the introspective, almost aimless nature of the crown chakra. Yet, when rooted in the crown chakra, this blend can produce a spiritual mentor who offers immense wisdom to the world. Such a mentor's authenticity stands out, primarily because their teachings emanate from the profound depths of the spiritual realm.

7–6

At the outset, this combination appears to lack an earthly grounding. Here, the third eye chakra draws its airy quality from the crown chakra while still harnessing its innate fiery essence.

Although this combination might not have the conventional tools for worldly expression, it shapes a spiritual scholar, one who dives deep and then surfaces with insights, striving to understand and articulate spiritual nuances. One could speculate that many philosopher-mystics throughout history possessed this intrinsic structure. They weren't content to solely reside on the spiritual plane; there was a compelling urge to elucidate, document, and intellectually dissect their transcendental experiences, as they aspired for spiritual wisdom.

The inherent dichotomy in this combination is tangible: the third eye chakra seeks understanding, while the crown chakra aims to transcend it. There might be internal struggles, but if spiritual experience remains the focal point, things will flow seamlessly. Shifting from a state of pure existence to one of comprehension, and from meditation to keen observation, offers immense potential. Embracing this natural trajectory not only aids personal growth but can illuminate the path for others, providing clarity in an often-mystifying spiritual landscape.

PART III
DIRECT YOUR INNER POWERS TOWARD FULFILLMENT

EIGHT

HARNESSING YOUR INNER POWERS

So far, you've learned how to identify your three dominant chakras, put them in the right order, and interpret the cosmic blueprint that defines you by examining the numbers and understanding how your three chakra personality types relate to each other. This journey has clarified your inner structure and enhanced your confidence in the arrangement of your chakra blueprint. Furthermore, your ability to understand the significance of the chakra blueprint system has grown immensely. You have built a strong foundation through the rigorous exercises in part II, and this final section of the book represents the culmination of your efforts. It's now time to relish the results and navigate the deeper dimensions using your chakra blueprint.

At an initial glance, this trio of numbers might appear to be of limited scope. However, as you journey through this book, these numbers transform from mere digits to foundational tools that assist in self-reflection and making life's crucial decisions. Truly understanding your personal blueprint goes beyond a one-time interpretation; it's about becoming your own guide—your personal astrologer, tarot reader, and numerologist. It's about tapping into the wisdom you hold within. By consistently engaging with your blueprint, you unearth insights and answers that are truly your own. The final part of this book will venture into this uncharted territory, aiding you on your journey of self-discovery.

Let's begin with a meditation centered on your three dominant chakras. In this practice, you will integrate the broader concept of "Chakra Flowering" (shared in chapter 1) into your personal alignment.

You can undertake this meditation with your eyes open or closed. If you opt for the latter, ensure that you familiarize yourself with the simple instructions provided first.

Practice

ALLOWING YOUR SOUL DESIGN TO BLOSSOM

Focus on the central channel where the chakras reside, gradually becoming attuned to the three dominant chakras that form your soul's design. Begin by concentrating on your primary chakra. Visualize a flower emerging from it, symbolizing its growth and vitality. Inhale deeply, directing your breath toward this primary chakra located deep within the central channel. As you continue breathing, envision the flower unfolding, its petals stretching out until they touch the front of your body. By facilitating the growth of your primary chakra, you're embracing the inherent essence of your personality, allowing it to shape and define your very existence. This essence becomes the fundamental lens through which you view and interact with the world, and it is now activated and vibrant.

Shift your focus to your secondary chakra, honing in on its energy point. Picture a flower (any that resonates with you) gradually unfurling from this chakra's core with each breath. It blossoms—initially timidly, then with confidence—stretching toward your body's front. Envision it shining in its full splendor. With both your primary and secondary chakras now luminous, sense their collective energy. By embracing the fullness of the secondary chakra, you channel the core of your being, actualizing your most genuine expression in the world.

Shift your attention to your supportive chakra, positioned in its precise energy spot. Visualize a flower symbolizing the growth of this center. As you deeply inhale into your supportive chakra, envision a bud emerging from the depth of the central channel, confidently revealing its petals and displaying its vibrant essence. It extends to the forefront of your body, radiating brilliantly. By allowing this supportive chakra to bloom, recognize the foundational support it provides for your life's path.

Take a deep breath, directing it toward these three flowers. Amplify their energy with each inhalation, sensing the interwoven roots that connect them. While they manifest as three distinct entities, they harmoniously operate as a single, unified flower. Gently conclude the meditation and softly open your eyes.

Happiness or Fulfillment?

How can you effectively harness the power of your three-type chakra structure to attain happiness, fulfillment, and balance? It's essential to note the sequence—happiness, fulfillment, and balance—as this represents the correct progression, especially once you grasp the nature of the three-type structure. The act of "harnessing" the power is crucial; it signifies that this structure offers insights beyond mere personality traits or preferences. It uncovers the three core energies or forces inherent in you, which guide your journey to true self-discovery and a fulfilling life.

Your primary, secondary, and supportive chakras are your intrinsic powers and energies. View them as sacred gifts from the cosmos, tailored for you to manifest and express your true destiny. Recognizing these forces as gifts intensifies empowerment. In this part of the book, I intend to help you connect with your framework and cherish it. When you acknowledge your inherent strengths, you will be awakened to the immense potentials within you. Your dominant chakras will guide you and allow you to direct your life's journey toward its zenith, much like a flower reaching full bloom (a sentiment captured in the "Chakra Flowering" meditation).

Each of us has three dominant chakras, but whether or not you utilize their power is up to you. If you remain clueless about channeling your dominant chakras, they can resemble three wild horses. Intended to guide and steer your soul's chariot, they instead pull in different directions, causing turmoil. To clarify, this analogy isn't originally mine but is inspired by Plato.[1] He employed it in a different setting, discussing harnessing your inner forces to nourish the soul, though the underlying message remains relevant. If you lack understanding and appreciation of these central forces, they don't just lose their harmony—they will propel you into a state of internal conflict. This misdirection results in contradiction and imbalance. Misunderstood forces can turn from strengths to vulnerabilities, even leading to self-destruction. Without awareness, these forces shift from conscious guides to subliminal— often destructive—internal influences.

For this very reason, understanding your inner structure is essential. When you fail to channel these energies appropriately, they stagnate, becoming a primary cause of conflict with others and life itself. This misdirection will often result in displaying the negative and imbalanced facets of your nature. In this state, for instance, a crown chakra type might spend most of their time resisting life's challenges, remaining vulnerable and unanchored rather than embracing the strength and blessings of their innate spirituality. Similarly, a heart chakra individual, a Caretaker, might turn into someone who is overwhelmingly emotionally reliant and persistently disappointed due to unrealistic expectations of others. This contrasts with their potential to be an emotional pillar radiating generosity, nurturance, and healing.

When I fail to harmonize my dominant chakra forces, I experience a significant drain in energy and an internal divide. This inner divide will be the central topic of this and subsequent chapters, given its importance. A key practice you'll explore, which you'll also come to understand and implement by the end of this chapter, involves visualizing yourself living in complete alignment with your inner structure. Through an in-depth visualization, you will create a palpable experience. Within this experience, you will start to discern how your awakened understanding of your structure can truly flourish in your life.

To enhance this visualization process, consider creating a vision board. This tool is a popular method that many utilize. With a vision board, you craft a collage, collecting images, symbols, and colors that represent your unique

---

1. Plato uses a similar analogy in his work *Phaedrus*.

goals. These visuals then steer your subconscious toward realization. In this context, you'll tailor the vision board to reflect your soul's design. (This will be discussed in detail later.) Together, the act of visualization and the vision board guide you in understanding the harmony of your three chakras. Instead of clashing, they become a fully realized and conscious gift in your life. The secret to unlocking these abilities lies in properly organizing your inner blueprint.

Picture your chakra blueprint, and envision how each of these three energy centers knows its rightful position. It's akin to roles in a company, dynamics in a romantic partnership, or members of a family: when every element recognizes its role, none attempts to dominate an area that isn't theirs. Each does its best, fulfilling its primary purpose, driven by a conscious desire to reinforce the overarching framework. This is the epitome of inner organization.

A crucial understanding you must have about your internal compass involves ensuring that self-fulfillment doesn't overshadow happiness, and vice versa. Often, people treat the concepts of self-fulfillment and happiness as one and the same. It's a common belief that we attain happiness when we feel fulfilled, and we associate it with success, creativity, recognition, or accomplishments. Society often paints a picture in which these are seen as synonymous with happiness. However, for many, fulfillment remains just that—fulfillment. Unless, perhaps, you align with the solar plexus chakra or throat chakra types, the Achiever or Speaker. For these types, happiness and fulfillment may indeed overlap significantly. But it's essential for the rest of the chakra types to recognize and separate these two notions.

Your primary chakra type is the wellspring of happiness, serving as the guardian of your most profound values. It's by aligning with your primary chakra type that you will truly feel in sync with the universe's grand design. In contrast, fulfillment represents the tangible manifestation of your inner happiness. It's how your internal sense of joy radiates outward. This distinction highlights that it's unwise to revel in happiness while forsaking fulfillment; doing so leaves an unsettling void of unmet potential. Likewise, an excessive emphasis on fulfillment at the expense of happiness results in a lingering sense of dissatisfaction and discontent. Individuals can achieve towering heights of success, wealth, or fame and yet be engulfed in a deep sense of unhappiness. This phenomenon isn't unfamiliar; tales abound of immensely successful individuals who, despite their achievements, remained steeped in sadness. Their plight may have stemmed from a lack of understanding of their inherent makeup and the inability to align with it.

There is a core strategy for actualizing your blueprint. First, you must firmly root yourself in your primary chakra type, anchoring your happiness. Simultaneously, channel your energies into your secondary chakra type, directing your fulfillment. This combination is the golden formula. To visualize this alignment, consider sketching it as a top-to-bottom flowchart. This not only lends clarity but also encapsulates the energy's descent from its inception in the primary chakra, cascading seamlessly down to result in tangible expression. Viewing your blueprint in this light lets you intuitively grasp the synchronicity and fluidity of your internal structure.

The concept of a downward flow often unveils intriguing patterns. Your blueprint might follow a sequence descending from higher to lower chakras, say 6–5–3, or it might trace the opposite trajectory, ascending from 4 to 5 and then 7. These patterns have significant meanings. With the downward sequence (6–5–3), we see a journey commencing from ethereal, spiritual realms toward tangible worldly expressions. Picture the fifth chakra (throat) as a conduit: it channels the illuminating energies from the third eye chakra into real-world goals and manifestations. This embodies the essence of flow. Contrarily, the upward sequence (4–5–7) suggests an evolution from earthly experiences toward spiritual ascension. Here, the journey starts with the fourth chakra, progresses through the fifth, and culminates in the spiritual realm of the seventh. This structure is like a spiritual magnet, pulling energies upward. It signifies an aspirational movement toward spiritual heights. It's as though the foundational love, expressed and refined, evolves into a higher spiritual yearning. This blueprint gravitates toward spiritual realms, whereas the downward sequence is rooted in material manifestation. In simpler terms, one blueprint gravitates toward the tangible, while the other seeks the spiritual.

Naturally, not every blueprint follows one direction. Some blueprints aim to achieve balance by integrating contrasting elements. Consider a 5–3–4 sequence that starts with a primary fifth chakra type, descends to a secondary third chakra type, and concludes with a supportive fourth chakra type. This blueprint does not have a straightforward flow in one direction but a harmonious interplay of opposites. Exploring such dimensions adds depth and provides further insight for understanding the interconnections within your blueprint.

Navigating Challenges Using Your Blueprint

In addition to differentiating between happiness and fulfillment and viewing your chakra structure as a cohesive flow, your chakra blueprint can help you make decisions and answer some of life's most profound questions. This method relies on a deep comprehension of the relationships between your three dominant chakras. When these interrelations are understood, they become a tool to address and dissolve some dilemmas and tensions you might encounter.

At times, you will grapple with inner conflict, perhaps even daily. As previously discussed, this tension typically arises between the primary and secondary chakra types as they struggle for dominance. However, it's not uncommon for the primary type to clash with both the secondary and supportive types. Occasionally, the discord may originate between the supportive type and the other two. Therefore, when assessing your blueprint, it's beneficial to remain receptive to these three potential sources of tension.

It's a fundamental aspect of human nature to experience conflicting desires. At times, this sensation might be so intense that you feel as if you are being pulled in different directions. Without proper alignment of your energetic framework, you will encounter division, confusion, and internal conflict. When you closely analyze your challenges, especially when you are facing a significant dilemma or conflicting desires, you'll recognize a pattern: when you're torn between wanting one thing and another, this indicates an underlying imbalance within your internal framework.

That's why gaining awareness of the persistent dilemmas and tensions in your life is vital. Simply acknowledging them as distinct desires isn't sufficient. You must actively discern these opposing inner voices and locate them within your personal chakra blueprint. This is crucial, for upon identifying them in your structure, you're equipped to understand, address, and resolve these contradictions.

With this heightened understanding, you may begin to question: *Does my secondary type lead me to believe that my joy is rooted in my sense of fulfillment? Have I unnecessarily intertwined my primary chakra life theme with that of my secondary type? Is there an external societal influence dictating my*

actions and expectations, one that doesn't align with my internal compass?
Could it be influenced by another chakra type in my surroundings? Your internal dialogue is pivotal to achieving clarity and order.

The Inner Oracle

Not only does the chakra blueprint help us differentiate between happiness and
fulfillment, it also aids in resolving internal discord. Now, imagine you have a
guiding force within you, one that is always ready to aid in decision-making or
answer your pressing questions. Think of this force as an internal oracle that
represents your chakra structure.

To tap into your internal oracle's wisdom, first think about your question.
Next, jot down your numbers sequentially (primary, secondary, supportive),
either from left to right or in expanding circles. If your query relates to fulfillment, a downward flowchart might be especially illuminating. Once you've
visualized your dominant chakras, pose your question to this intrinsic structure and listen attentively. The answers to your soul's inquiries already reside
within your chakra constellation. Think of your blueprint as a celestial key,
given to you and waiting to be utilized. By consistently engaging with this
structure, remaining true to it, and making it a central guide in your life,
you can continuously revisit it at various junctures. Doing so, you'll uncover
deeper insights that help clarify your soul's purpose in this lifetime: understanding your identity, discerning your destiny, recognizing your intended
role, and actualizing your capabilities. However, while answers to life's questions have roots in your blueprint, they aren't immutable. The answers are
fluid, continually changing and adapting with your personal evolution. As
you grow and mature, your insights will evolve too.

By grasping your inner structure, you align with your intended path and
what might be termed a higher purpose. This alignment grants you the serenity to settle into your unique place in the vast mosaic of existence. Beauty lies
in realizing that by embracing your distinct role, you don't stand apart but
rather seamlessly blend into the cosmic narrative. Such awareness illuminates your integral connection to the universe and your intrinsic worth in the
greater plan.

It's crucial to recognize that every chakra type holds significance in the
world, and each structure is valuable to society. One of the most enlightening

questions you can ask yourself is *How can my chakra blueprint benefit and serve those around me and the broader world?* Think of this as the voice of your structure; when approached in this manner, its purpose becomes abundantly clear.

We've covered three applications so far: distinguishing between happiness and fulfillment, resolving internal conflict, and aiding in decision-making and finding answers. A fourth application (identifying potential pitfalls and self-sabotaging tendencies within the structure) will be elaborated on in the book's final section. Equipped with these applications, you can begin to explore the art of maintaining a conscious equilibrium. Achieving balance is rooted in three foundational elements: a nurturing environment, uplifting companionship, and personal introspection. Interestingly, these elements are tied to the four absent chakras. Through this perspective, you're guided to moderate your excesses while addressing your shortcomings. In essence, balance is about recognizing where you overflow and where you're lacking—a crucial consideration in your journey.

The fifth and final application, which will be addressed in chapter 11, revolves around the design of a tailored coaching program. This program aligns with your chakra structure, but it can be adjusted to serve the needs of friends and loved ones if you choose to share these methods. A coaching program can aid others in navigating deficiencies and maximizing their three inherent powers. Above all, it illuminates the path toward a harmonious manifestation. Remember, this can only be achieved once all three types collaborate smoothly to support the overarching structure, a state where three distinct parts have come together as a unified whole. This mirrors the "Chakra Flowering" practice: if each of the three chakras is allowed to blossom, they will merge as one radiant flower.

This concludes your introduction to the five applications. Now, you can begin to incorporate these principles in the practices found in the remainder of the book.

You are about to embark on a journey of expansion. The practices in this chapter are exceptionally beneficial, as they allow you to directly experience your chakra types and structure, rather than seeing the chakras as mere objects of inquiry or numerical representations. These direct interactions with your energetic blueprint provide insight into its fully realized form.

The essence of expansion is to recognize and awaken the latent capabilities within, bringing everything from potentiality into actuality.

Practice
• • • • • •
EXPANDING YOUR SECONDARY CHAKRA TYPE

You can follow the straightforward guidelines in this practice to enhance any of the chakras in your soul design. This can be highly beneficial, not only for familiarizing yourself with your structure but also for identifying the correct order through your awakened inner eye. Nevertheless, this practice's emphasis is on expanding the secondary chakra type.

As previously noted, the secondary chakra can serve two main roles: first, as a balancer, and second, as a fulfillment enabler. Awakening the middle of the structure ensures that the entire structure remains balanced. Additionally, in its role as a fulfillment enabler, activating the secondary chakra serves as a crucial aid in the decision-making processes. This activation helps with making the right choices in life, defining your next steps, and shaping your future. You will be pleasantly surprised by the profound clarity you will gain from this state!

The process of expansion begins by focusing on amplifying the secondary chakra type. As you engage with this robust and highly active energy center, you will begin to give it some definition, using your senses to identify its location in the body. While the location of your secondary chakra may already be known to you, surprises may emerge during this experience. Next, you will initiate expansion. This entails visualizing the enlargement of the identified pattern. For example, if you experience the throat chakra type as a blue bridge in the midst of an ocean, you would begin to visualize this pattern deep within your throat chakra, allowing it to grow larger using your intention, force of visualization, and breathing. After you amplify the image and pattern as much as possible, you will allow yourself to unveil its deeper, broader, or more spiritual essence. This process is used to reach an expanded level of consciousness that reveals the more meaningful potential of your type.

You will repeat this process time and time again. In fact, you will undergo this process four times, executing four expansions. In this regard, the procedure is repetitive, serving to broaden both your vision and your consciousness. With every cycle of expansion, your experience of your chakra type will deepen and refine.

Allocate at least thirty minutes for this practice. Naturally, if you feel the need for additional time, do not hesitate to take it.

1. Sit in a comfortable position and close your eyes. Allow your entire being to relax gradually. Breathe slowly and deeply.

2. Through this relaxation, get in touch with the essence of your secondary chakra type, which governs the expression of your three-type structure. Feel it as an energy emanating from you, a power that helps you bring your desires to fruition.

3. Breathe into the essence of your secondary chakra. Move into its depth, into its very core. Try to communicate it—what does it feel like? Look for the area in the body that is most connected to your secondary chakra. Do you see the chakra as a shape or an image? A color? A general sensation or a fragrance?

4. Now breathe into the essence of your secondary chakra and feel it from within. Let it spread further, permeating your entire body and being. Breathe into the shape or image and into its area in the body. Breathe into it and let it expand more and more until it reaches its limit, until it cannot expand any more. Say, "[Secondary chakra type], show yourself completely to me!"

5. Breathe into the expanded essence. Move into its very core. Try to communicate it—what does it feel like? Look for the area in the body that is most connected to this state. Do you see the essence as a shape or an image? A color? A general sensation or a fragrance? Finally, give a name to the expanded essence.

6. Now, breathe into the expanded essence and feel it from within. Let it spread further, permeating your entire body and being. Breathe into the shape or image and into its area in the body.

Breathe and let it expand more and more until it reaches its limit, until it cannot expand any more. Say, "[Expanded essence], show yourself completely to me!"

7. Breathe into this new state. Move into its very core. Try to communicate it—what does it feel like? Look for the area in the body that is most connected to this state. Do you see this state as a shape or an image? A color? A general sensation or a fragrance? Give a name to this new expanded state.

8. Now, breathe in the expanded state and feel it from within. Let it spread further, permeating your entire body and being. Breathe into the shape or image and into its area in the body; breathe and let it expand more and more until it reaches its limit, until it cannot expand any more. Say, "[Expanded state], show yourself completely to me!"

9. Repeat steps 7 and 8 once more.

10. Breathe into this state. Move into its very core. Try to communicate it—what does it feel like? What does the expanded essence of your secondary chakra type enable you to understand about the higher potential of your self-fulfillment? How would you live and express yourself based on this expanded chakra type essence? What happens to the entire three-type structure when the secondary type is expanded and awakened? Express gratitude toward your secondary chakra type for being your guiding light on your journey toward self-fulfillment.

11. As much as possible, allow this expanded state to permeate your physical body from head to toe. Before you open your eyes, you can choose to remain in touch with this state through your heart, even in your ordinary state of consciousness. Slowly and gently open your eyes.

Practice

· · • • • • ·

VISUALIZING THE BLOSSOMING OF YOUR SOUL DESIGN

This exercise is a visualization in which you will start to shape a vivid image of your soul design at its peak bloom. The more intricate this image, the more impactful it becomes. It's comparable to sowing seeds in your subconscious, or better yet, drawing out elements from the subconscious and presenting them to your conscious awareness. This visualization will play a vital role in chapter 11, when it serves as the groundwork for your coaching approach. For now, the priority is to cultivate this inner clarity.

For optimal results, I recommended jotting down your thoughts during the visualization. So, have a pen and paper or a digital document ready. As you meditate, pause occasionally to record your visions, emotions, and sensations. You'll find these notes invaluable later on.

The visualization process is divided into five steps, with each step enriching and intensifying the imagery. Once you've read the instructions for each phase, I recommend closing your eyes to deepen your visualization experience, if that is comfortable for you.

Align

1. Inhale deeply and exhale slowly. Begin to ease your body and mind. Approach this visualization journey with joy and curiosity. It's a partnership between your subconscious and conscious realms. Visualize the three numbers of your structure or, if you have written them down, peek at them before shutting your eyes once more.

   Start by picturing your life in complete harmony with your primary chakra type—not considering all aspects, but focusing solely on aligning and merging with this central chakra. Dive deep into this visualization, exploring behaviors, actions, emotions, and presence. How would living in sync with your primary chakra manifest and resonate? Reflect on this, and

whenever insights arise that you'd like to note, take a moment
to record them.

Integrate

2. Now, gently incorporate your secondary chakra type into your
visualization, ensuring that you remain rooted in the primary
chakra. Next, layer in the supportive chakra type, all the while
maintaining the focus on your primary chakra type. Observe
the changes and nuances that emerge as you integrate these
additional chakra types. What shifts do you notice?

Envision

3. Imagine a life led by your fully awakened three-type structure.
How does it appear and resonate when you live in tune with
this enlightened understanding of your composition?

Explore

4. How does it manifest when these three types operate in seamless unity and harmony? As you let this vision unfold, take
note if any lingering questions you hold. Find their answers
effortlessly.

Investigate

5. Lastly, after envisioning life in its entirety, delve into its various facets. Investigate how these aspects will be influenced
by your harmonized three-type structure. This exploration
might touch upon your daily habits, eating patterns, practices,
interpersonal relationships, and many other areas.

* * * * * * *

Great job! I'm confident that this visualization has provided you with valuable insight. Transforming what has been discussed into a visualization
brings that knowledge to life, allowing you to observe its flow, behavior, and
action. You might have stumbled upon a revelation, a surprising insight, or
even something that reaffirmed or strengthened your prior discoveries.

NINE

EMBRACING YOUR PRIMARY TYPE

Now I want to address a pivotal point, which is truly at the heart of the entire chakra types method. Grasping this concept can empower you to interpret and utilize blueprints in profound and impactful ways. I'm sure you've noticed I emphasized a specific principle on multiple occasions throughout this book: the idea of settling into your primary type. Embracing your primary type is a foundational solution that introduces order, unity, and harmony to your whole structure. Take a moment to resonate with the sensation of settling into your primary type. My choice of words is intentional: *settling into, easing yourself into*.

In the previous chapter, you visualized a life fully aligned with the three-chakra type structure. You may have noticed that the visualization approach didn't directly dive into the triadic structure. This is because the life journey within this framework starts with your primary chakra type. From this core, life unfolds and evolves, with the primary type always acting as your unwavering anchor. This center is always intact. Thus, the initial emphasis was on amplifying the growth of the primary type, followed by the integration of the secondary and finally the supportive chakra type.

It's time to devote an entire chapter to this profound insight, exploring it from varied angles. My aim is for this principle to resonate deeply within you, enabling you to navigate your blueprint and discover solutions with increased clarity. A recurring theme you'll encounter when seeking answers or making decisions based on your blueprint is this: always start by grounding yourself in your primary chakra type. In essence, this statement will be the cornerstone of all solutions. Its significance is monumental. But why is it so crucial? It boils down to this: if your primary type remains unsettled and its values are dismissed or disregarded, other strategies will fail. If you don't acknowledge and embrace this foundation, true contentment will always elude you, no matter the path chosen.

You Are a Manifestation of a Cosmic Pattern

In the end, the chakra types method is rooted in a central purpose: understanding and accepting who you genuinely are. That's the journey here—to recognize and embody your authentic identity. If you recall, in the introduction I addressed a piece of feedback I often hear regarding the chakra types. Some argue that being labeled feels restricting; they oppose being pigeonholed. However, such feelings originate from one's self-perception, not the tangible truth of who one is. Self-image is your idealized view of yourself, while reality paints a picture of your true nature. So, who do you truly stand to be?

In reality, your thoughts, feelings, and experiences follow distinct patterns, making you more predictable than you might believe. Over time, others can anticipate my reactions based on how I interpret the world around me. Similarly, your perceptions and reactions are uniquely yours, distinct from mine. This is the undeniable truth. We are manifestations of cosmic patterns.

While human beings easily accept that roses differ from sunflowers, we struggle to accept our own individual patterns. Many believe that they can become anything and everything simultaneously. This mindset is not only far from reality but also an impediment to recognizing your intrinsic nature. This reluctance keeps you from truly embracing and expressing your unique qualities and strengths, the very attributes you're designed to contribute to the world.

Each of us possesses a destiny. It might not be a grand saga like *The Lord of the Rings*, but your destiny is a distinctive pattern that you're meant to unfold, enabling it to reach its full potential as a reflection of your cosmic nature. While the chakra-type structure doesn't pinpoint your exact destiny—indeed, no method can—it guides your energy, passion, and skills toward the path the universe has paved for you. In essence, the method illuminates your intended role and direction in life.

There are a few individuals who might not rely on the method as much. This is because they exude a natural clarity and distinction. They don't necessarily need a blueprint handed to them; they embody it. Their presence is like a storm, a direct reflection of their intrinsic structure. While this knowledge might still offer them a deeper alignment or increased contentment, they inherently tread a path that is evident to them without much effort.

I've emphasized the importance of recognizing the primary chakra type as your center, but do not bind yourself to it as if it's a new flag to wave or a political party to pledge allegiance to. The spiritual journey encourages you to move beyond rigid identities. My goal isn't to box you in or limit your understanding of self. This misunderstanding arises if you view the chakra types as an identity. Instead, consider your dominant chakra types as a conduit for expression and realization, an efficient means to articulate and achieve fulfillment.

Once you've grasped this concept, revisit what I mentioned in the previous chapter: embracing your primary type is not just about categorization; it's about syncing with your purpose and deciphering your unique role in the vast cosmos. Alignment feels like stepping into your true position, as your primary chakra type mirrors the way life desires to express itself through you. This journey is about valuing and sharing the gifts you hold. The perspective offered by your primary chakra type is one that others require, embodying a special form of wisdom. By wholeheartedly dedicating yourself to this wisdom, you radiate an authentic and inspirational life.

If each individual consciously aligned with and lived by the guiding principles of their primary chakra type, allowing this richness to ripple outward to those around them and society at large, we could envision a transformed humanity. This understanding paves the way for building conscious organizations, teams, and communities. (For those identified as Speakers, these thoughts likely resonate deeply.) However, even when establishing structures where everyone operates within their chakra roles, it's crucial to use discretion. You must avoid falling into the trap of judging or stereotyping individuals based on their chakra types rather than appreciating the value they bring. The path to a renewed humanity can be found by acknowledging each person's unique cosmic imprint and genuinely exploring how their intrinsic qualities can contribute to the collective.

Consider, for instance, the sacral chakra type, the Artist. They infuse vibrancy into every setting, offering gifts of aesthetics, beauty, and a keen sense of the present moment. They are distinguished by their innovative and unexpected ideas combined with their profound connection to nature. However, the specifics of their influence can vary based on their individual makeup. Some exude boundless joy and energy, while others might embody the intense and tumultuous spirit of a creative. Rather than criticizing what they lack in comparison to others, you should embrace and lean into their strengths, allowing their unique qualities to enhance and complete your collective or organizational dynamics.

The Key to Self-Love

In this context, the primary chakra can be viewed as the chakra of self-acceptance or self-love. To truly embrace oneself means to fully align with one's primary type. It's important to note that the journey to self-acceptance is personal; it's not about seeking approval or understanding from others. Only you have the power and responsibility to accept and understand yourself.

Let me pose a question: do you embrace who you are? Whether you're a heart chakra type or a solar plexus chakra type, do you cherish that aspect of yourself, or do you feel burdened by it? Do you see it as a blessing? It's essential to truly appreciate your primary chakra type. This isn't about categorizing yourself or building an identity around your primary chakra, but rather recognizing and valuing the unique gifts you possess.

Understanding yourself is pivotal. It demands such profound intimacy with your own essence that you never stray from the path inherently meant for you. No longer will you diverge simply because someone else wants you to fit their mold or appease their desires. Cultivating this clarity requires a unique depth of self-confidence, which the blueprint system seeks to instill within you.

Once you're sure of your identity, the path to self-acceptance unfolds. You will start to become comfortable with your individuality. But this self-awareness is only the beginning. As you truly accept yourself, feelings of self-worth and value emerge, culminating in robust self-confidence. With this innate understanding of who you are, there's no reason to adopt another's persona to thrive in the world.

Remember, your type isn't a construct of your own creation. It's the brainchild of the universe's greatest architect, whether you refer to this force as existence, the cosmos, or God. This mastermind envisioned your unique identity and intended for you to embrace it. Your role is simply to recognize and become conscious of this design. Once you resonate with your dominant chakra types and abandon the pursuit of being someone else, you will find yourself intertwined with the life force that also manifested flowers, giraffes, koalas, beetles, the grandeur of black holes, supernovas, and emerging stars. Really, would you dare question this cosmic brilliance?

As I briefly mentioned in part II, whenever you grapple with feelings of dissatisfaction or sense that your soul is yearning for more, it's often because you're not living a life authentic to yourself. Instead, you're living a life misaligned with who you truly are, especially in relation to your primary chakra type. It's crucial to evaluate how to strengthen this bond. This connection is your link to the grand design of the universe.

Certainly, another source of dissatisfaction could be feeling that you aren't fully showcasing your primary chakra type's potential. This sentiment might also encompass the secondary type due to the underlying frustration with expression. However, at its core, this issue ties back to the primary chakra type, which acts as the focal point. The heart of the matter is the perceived gap between your current expression and the potential depth of your primary chakra type.

If you believe that your discontentment stems from a lack of nourishment, linking it to the supportive chakra type, consider this: it still ultimately ties back to your primary chakra type. Your underlying concern is that the primary type isn't receiving sufficient energy to fully manifest. While this energy is undeniably essential, its ultimate purpose is to empower the primary type. Everything converges to that singular focus.

The Key to Resolving Inner Struggles

From what has been discussed thus far, it's evident that identifying with your primary chakra type is the key to alleviating inner tensions and conflicts within your soul design. Keep in mind that your fundamental tensions and challenges are primarily the result of interactions between your dominant chakras. However, once the entire system recognizes that the primary chakra type is the guiding force and every other chakra's expression is an extension of it, a harmonious balance is achieved. This allows for the integration of the entire structure into a cohesive whole.

This idea mirrors a widely recognized belief. Many perceive their minds as barriers to genuine freedom and authenticity. However, the issue isn't the mind itself, but rather when it assumes a dominant role in existence. Conversely, when the mind takes a back seat, letting the heart drive, a balance is struck. Similarly, the supplementary chakras should act in support of the primary chakra. Embracing this function leads to a beautiful alignment.

I trust you're beginning to grasp why the visualization technique covered in the previous chapter started by anchoring yourself in the primary chakra type before exploring the constellation of all three. Similarly, when drafting your life's vision board (which will be explored in chapter 11), it's vital to use the primary chakra type as its cornerstone. Beginning with this foundational perspective significantly enriches the entire visualization process.

In wrapping up this topic, I'd like to emphasize that truly embracing your primary type means more than just recognizing its inherent beauty and the value it brings to your life. It's also about acknowledging and accepting its core challenges and imbalances.

Recall the life theme or the inherent struggle associated with each primary chakra type. When I introduced the forty-two combinations of the primary and secondary types, I noted that a select few have structures where the secondary chakra type significantly counteracts the primary type's challenges. Some combinations naturally and seamlessly offset the typical imbalances found in the primary chakra. For instance, if someone with a root chakra as their primary type has a sacral chakra as their secondary type, this pairing often alleviates many of the root chakra's issues. Similarly, a primary throat chakra paired with a secondary root chakra can neutralize many challenges commonly associated with the throat chakra.

Many of us aren't fortunate enough to have complementary chakras that effortlessly balance each other out. Often, life's themes can be intensified or complicated due to your unique chakra structure, especially when other chakras vie for dominance. This inevitably means more inner work for you.

However, it's crucial to remember not to adopt the life themes of your secondary chakra. Understand that their themes aren't your primary responsibility. Grappling with one life theme is challenging enough! You must ensure that your secondary chakra doesn't lead you astray; while it can contribute to your overall happiness and sense of meaning, it shouldn't define your primary life theme. It isn't directly connected to it.

In essence, it's vital to grasp the life theme deeply rooted in the imbalances of your primary chakra type, and to accept it as your soul's challenge. You have a duty to confront and navigate this central tension with intentional self-reflection. If you neglect this essential theme, your foundational structure may stagnate as it is burdened by unresolved issues. Ignoring these issues can turn life into a never-ending battle, which will deplete your inherent energy. For a harmonious existence, you must ensure that energy flows freely, beginning at the core and radiating outward through the secondary and supportive channels. Once the primary chakra adequately addresses its life theme, the entire blueprint progresses toward realizing its aspirations, and it does so while grounded in a state of contentment, joy, and wholeness.

In the next chapter, you will begin to practice, pose questions, and navigate decisions using the chakra blueprint, and the importance of this chapter will become even more evident. You'll realize that proper inner alignment is key—without it, clarity will remain elusive. Everything depends on this foundational positioning.

TEN

ANSWERING LIFE'S
BIG QUESTIONS

You're heading into the final lessons that are essential for understanding the three chakra–type structure. In this chapter, a lot is covered, from universal principles to your own journey of discovery. You've learned how to harness your blueprint in your daily life, and you see the three types not just as personality traits, but as energies or powers that you can align and direct. In this chapter, you'll learn methods to do just that.

These methods have been touched on in previous chapters. Once again, the four methods are:

1. Settling into the primary chakra as the touchstone for every choice and decision.

2. Recognizing and deciphering core challenges and tensions, perceiving them as interplays between your three dominant chakras.

3. Expanding your secondary chakra, which is the fulfillment chakra, when you seek to align the system and steer it toward completion.

4. Envisioning a life that resonates seamlessly with your internal framework.

Now, how might the chakra blueprint serve as a tool for alleviating internal conflict, answering life's big questions, and refining the decision-making processes? This exploration will take place toward the end of the chapter in a practice called Resolving Questions and Dilemmas. This practice will illuminate how to effectively integrate the principles and practices you've learned in part III.

Before you dive into that practice, here is a short meditation to deeply connect to your chakra type.

Practice
. . . .

TRACING YOUR SOUL'S BLUEPRINT

Close your eyes, take a deep breath, and relax into a meditative state. Focus on the central column inside the body, just in front of the spine, stretching from the base all the way to the top of the head. Here, you can sense different energy centers deep within you. Three of these centers are especially strong and vibrant.

Now, think about where these energy patterns come from. These patterns fuel your strongest feelings and ways of interacting with life. Imagine tracing these three energy patterns back to their source. Where do they begin? Try to feel the profound mystery behind your structure and the pure essence from which it emerges. Look deeply into the origin of your own unique design.

. . . .

To set the stage for the Resolving Questions and Dilemmas practice, we need to revisit the principle of interpreting a blueprint. Prior lessons centered around creating a foundational personality analysis. Now, the aim is to uncover additional applications of your blueprint. These methods become meaningful only after you've undergone a thorough (or at minimum, an introductory) analysis of your chakra blueprint.

Using your foundational analysis as a stepping stone, you're empowered to undertake any of the following actions whenever necessary, not just as a one-time endeavor:

- You have the ability to reconcile internal conflicts and conflicting voices.
- You can seek answers to questions about your life's path. These queries might range from broad and fundamental to incredibly detailed and specific.
- You can make choices that align with your inherent structure.

The varied applications of the blueprint highlight its everyday relevance. Essentially, these three actions merge into one holistic process. When making a decision, for example, it's crucial to address inner conflicts and to recognize inherent contradictions. Subsequently, one must learn how to formulate the right questions and remain receptive to the answers.

Though these three actions intertwine, there are moments when the focus is on introspection rather than decision-making. At times, you may find yourself overwhelmed by a search for inner clarity. In such moments, one approach is to articulate—whether in writing or aloud—all the internal debates and conflicts you're experiencing. It's intriguing to identify these disparate voices: one might be encouraging, another doubtful, and perhaps a third, fourth, or even fifth adding to the cacophony. It's somewhat astonishing to recognize the multitude of selves within! The key is to distinctly define each voice and its message. With that clarity, the next step is to understand the origins of the contradictory voices. As previously mentioned, these voices stem from the three dominant chakra types, which can clash and conflict when unaligned, behaving less like allies and more like adversaries.

Your three dominant chakras are essentially life partners, bound together within a single framework. They're intended to work in unison. Yet when they behave as separate entities or compete for dominance, it disrupts your inner balance. Identifying the messages of each dominant chakra will illuminate the situation vividly. In fact, achieving this clarity is often half the battle.

This process can be particularly useful for addressing and understanding internal conflicts. The initial step is to identify conflicting inner voices and discern their origins, pinpointing which chakra type each resonates with. Once you've located the sources of your inner dialogue, it is imperative to recognize that every solution begins by aligning with and showing loyalty to your primary chakra type. This alignment offers clarity and provides a solid foundation. From this grounded stance, the other two chakra types harmonize and operate with efficacy. They are designed to support and assist the primary type. Likewise, the primary chakra type leans on these secondary types for enrichment, nourishment, and empowerment. Yet, at the heart of it all, it's the primary chakra type that must find contentment and joy. Your primary type serves as the bridge to the meaning of life, guiding you to your destined role and rightful place in the world. If it remains unfulfilled, a sense of harmony will evade you. Solutions favoring your secondary or supportive chakras will eventually fall short, leading to feelings of bitterness and the sensation of life slipping through your fingers. It's vital to understand that true satisfaction is anchored in your primary chakra type.

Now that we've discussed the guiding principle of loyalty to the primary chakra type, turn your attention to the numbers. Continuously observe their interplay, noting their relationships and any underlying tensions. This method fosters a genuine dialogue with the numbers. Before introducing this approach to others, it's wise to refine it through repeated self-application. Once you've consistently derived meaningful answers for yourself, you can confidently share this tool with others. Naturally, this assumes that guiding others in this manner resonates with your chakra structure.

The third stage asks you to evaluate your intuitive response. Determine whether the solution to your inner conflict would establish a harmonious rhythm and flow in your internal framework. Are all chakras correctly aligned and functioning? Do they seamlessly transition from essence to fulfillment? When considering the solution, does it bring you a sense of contentment? Does it resonate deeply, making you feel completely in tune with your authentic self?

Engaging with your chakra blueprint essentially awakens your inner guru. By maintaining a continuous dialogue with your innate structure, you're aligning yourself with your soul's journey and cosmic intention. Your blueprint bridges the gap between you and a higher purpose. The more attuned and attentive you are, the more your blueprint reveals, providing you with increased clarity. When you assist others, you're not merely answering their questions—you're guiding them to connect with their own inner guru, facilitating their self-realization. That's the profound impact you will have.

As you approach the final steps of resolving inner conflict, it's crucial to validate the solution's completeness and correctness using visualization. After pinpointing your solution, shut your eyes. Vividly imagine living or behaving in alignment with that solution. This will offer you deep insight into its harmony with your essence. How does the solution resonate within your body, your natural compass for authenticity and falsehood? What is its energetic vibe? Do you feel at ease, fulfilled, integrated, or content? How does this solution reshape your actions?

Visualization lends a practical and tangible layer to the solution, and it can be a shared experience with someone seeking your guidance. The goals of incorporating visualization are:

- To confirm the authenticity and precision of the response, resulting in intuitive, tangible feedback.
- To foster a connection between the depths of your subconscious (or the soul's intuition) and your conscious mind, which creates a genuine sense of alignment.

As you engage in this mental journey, it's wise to document your feelings and insights, either during the process or immediately afterward.

Be Inspired by This Example

Before diving into the Resolving Questions and Dilemmas practice, I'd like to offer an illustrative example. Let's explore how I might address a question posed by someone with a primary sacral chakra, a secondary heart chakra, and a supportive throat chakra. Observe the sequence: 2–4–5.

In this scenario, a man seeks my advice regarding a pressing relationship dilemma: whether to stay or leave. Considering his specific alignment, he is inclined to describe the relationship as both loving and, paradoxically, constricting and limiting.

My immediate instinct is to dissect the dilemma, tracing it back to its fundamental conflict. It's essential to revert the question to its internal drivers, as these intrinsic forces are often at the heart of such dilemmas. The crux of my approach lies in identifying the tension's origin, which is rooted in the interplay of his chakra structure.

As I converse with the man, I inquire about his typical behaviors and feelings in relationships. Through this discussion, I reaffirm patterns and structures identified in previous relationships. Remarkably, these patterns consistently validate themselves across all aspects of life. They're present in every conflict and dilemma we face.

It's evident to me that the man's solution lies in fully embodying his primary chakra identity: the sacral chakra, referred to as the Artist. While considering this, it's vital to recognize the role of the heart chakra in the Artist's fulfillment, adding layers to the situation. Examining the chakra system further, I note the presence of the throat chakra. I find that in this context, this chakra holds lesser importance and is not crucial to the discussion.

What emerges is a defining interplay between the sacral and heart chakras. The heart chakra—the man's fulfillment center—urges him toward deeper connections, devotion, and sometimes prioritizing others over himself. On the other hand, the sacral chakra champions a sense of independence and a less intense commitment, as it is more about sensuality than profound emotional connections. However, it's crucial to remember that ultimate fulfillment lies in the secondary chakra. In this case, that is the heart chakra type.

The heart chakra type signifies a deep-rooted dependence on such fulfillment that he can't escape. Throughout his life, the man will naturally gravitate toward relationships, deep emotional ties, and shared connections; these elements are inescapable. Yet his chakra structure doesn't impose a singular, monogamous connection. Instead, he may be drawn to evolving dynamics, diverse interactions, or nontraditional relationship structures.

It's worth noting that the sacral chakra's essence is channeled primarily through the heart; this implies its manifestation in emotional connections rather than in rigid structures. In reality, fluidity is more aligned with this type than any fixed framework.

The bad news is that this chakra structure seems destined to navigate a lifetime of relational challenges. The internal struggle ingrained in the man's blueprint means that he is perpetually longing for what he currently lacks. When single, he might unconsciously yearn for an ideal partner; yet, even in the embrace of a loving relationship, he may crave independence or the thrill of a different companion.

However, the primary sacral chakra is deeply rooted in the realm of experience. It highlights the fleeting aspect of expression and the pursuit of deep, meaningful moments. No intense experience lasts forever, does it? This fleetingness is inherent in the very definition of experience. For Artists, every interaction is fundamentally an experience, and even the most captivating moments have their endpoint. Since emotional ties for this chakra type are closely linked to feelings of contentment or its absence, it's crucial to stay true to the sacral chakra's nature. This suggests that the man's true loyalty lies in being genuine to himself. That's the essence of faithfulness in this context.

This authenticity might not align with social norms. Some chakra structures are inclined to equate commitment with mature love, leading them to assume that those with a primary sacral chakra type are incapable of love in the sense that they can't pledge lifelong commitment to one individual. However, the chakra types system suggests that love's definition varies for each of us. There is no reason to follow society's prescription of a one-size-fits-all approach to love. For example, love can exist without sexual components or even outside the confines of a partnership. So, my counsel would be for the man to free himself from societal expectations that don't align with his unique chakra structure. After all, nowhere in his blueprint does it state that he must love in a predefined manner.

Essentially, this chakra structure requires relationships, but they must be relationships that allow considerable freedom. Only with this liberty can connections thrive. Unconventional relationship structures such as polyamory usually align well with this framework. A lifelong, singular commitment might be challenging, and if attempted, it will only prosper if it is free from definitions or expectations. Any binding relationship will inevitably induce feelings of confinement, leading to resistance. Thus, if the man's partner cannot provide the space he needs, it might be best to end the relationship. If his only options are a strictly monogamous, unwavering bond or no relationship at all, I would doubt the relationship's feasibility.

The man should remain resolute and champion his distinct way of loving. This doesn't necessarily imply an abrupt end of the relationship. Instead, he could suggest a profound change to the relationship's dynamics, expressing the need for space and love that flows without restriction. However, if such adjustments don't resonate with his partner, it may be best to move on. Importantly, this choice serves the man's well-being *and* his partner's, who might have shouldered the weight of this discord for a long time. (Whenever we assess a relationship, we ought to consider those close to us who have grappled with our internal conflicts for extended periods. Taking responsibility for this is essential.)

This analysis has served as a demonstration of my method for interpreting the blueprint of an individual who has posed a question to me. This was simply a glimpse of how one might approach such a process. As you engage with others' blueprints, I hope you find the journey to be playful, creative, and genuinely enjoyable.

Practice
• • • • • • •
RESOLVING QUESTIONS AND DILEMMAS

Now, you're prepared to enhance your analytical skills and address questions using a chakra blueprint. This exercise will be deliberate and thorough, advancing carefully from one stage to the next so you can skillfully tackle questions and dilemmas. You'll journey through six distinct phases. During each one, you'll be prompted to take notes, so ensure you're equipped with either pen and paper or a digital document.

Listening

Set aside five minutes to begin the practice.

1. Begin by identifying a question you aim to address, a choice you're pondering, or an internal dilemma. Everyone grapples with such challenges, whether they're acutely aware of them or not. At times, pressing questions will occupy your thoughts, whereas on other occasions, questions will be obscured by the day's unresolved feelings and concerns. This is why you're setting aside five minutes to pinpoint and articulate your particular challenge. Embrace this moment.

   If it helps, jot down some preliminary thoughts on your situation before focusing on your primary inquiry. Then, crystallize the central issue or choice at hand. By the time five minutes have passed, aim to have your dilemma distilled into a clear statement or question.

Recognizing

Set aside ten minutes for this task.

2. Start by documenting all of the internal dialogue related to your dilemma. Capture the conflicts and contradictions you feel. Articulate contrasting feelings and thoughts with as much detail as you can. Recognizing all your internal voices demands careful attention and thorough exploration.

Organizing

Devote at least ten minutes to this portion of the exercise.

3. Review what you've written. Next, draw three columns. Write your chakra sequence over the top of the columns, with the primary chakra type ruling the left column, the secondary chakra in the middle, and the supportive chakra on the right.

   Now, return to your writing and identify the chakra type associated with each voice. Begin to align the voices and the chakras in the appropriate column. This arrangement will bring clarity to which internal voice corresponds with which chakra.

   As you organize, feel free to add any additional statements or voices that come to mind.

Revealing

This step will take about ten minutes. Feel free to take more time if you need it.

4. Begin by recognizing that every solution is rooted in your primary chakra type. With this foundation, examine the three numbers and their interconnections. Engage with the three numbers while reflecting on your initial dilemma. Let the solution reveal itself.

Examining

Once you have reached a solution, set aside five minutes to examine it.

5. Reflect on your solution. Does it ensure a harmonious flow in line with your soul design? Are all three chakra types correctly positioned and fulfilling their roles? Is there a clear flow from essence to tangible realization? Does this solution resonate with your true self, bringing feelings of contentment and joy?

    Pause for a moment and examine your solution. Consider your internal framework and allow yourself to deeply connect with these insights.

Visualizing

This final portion of the exercise will take about ten minutes.

6. Close your eyes and vividly imagine living your life based on this solution. As this scene unfolds in your mind, ask yourself: Does it resonate harmoniously? How does your body react to it? What's the energy like? Do you feel at peace, complete, and content? Would this solution inspire a change in your actions? Write down your observations now or right after completing this visualization.

    As you reach the conclusion of this process, immerse yourself in a detailed visualization of your life, particularly the way you conduct yourself based on this newfound insight. Reflect on the harmony of this vision. Tune in to the sensations in your body and its energetic aura, ensuring that it evokes feelings of comfort, wholeness, and fulfillment. Ponder whether this guidance nudges you to act differently.

    Continue refining your vision, striving for alignment and harmony both physically and energetically to ensure that your proposed way of life genuinely aligns with your core values.

    When you are ready, gently open your eyes.

In this practice, you attempted to find a solution to a dilemma using your chakra blueprint. This was a comprehensive practice, and as such, it should have taken approximately fifty minutes. Given the potential to resolve or shed light on a pressing dilemma, this time investment is quite reasonable, especially when compared to the countless hours or days you might otherwise spend in uncertainty. That said, with practice, you might find that you can complete the process in as little as thirty to forty minutes.

Practice
HELPING SOMEONE ELSE RESOLVE QUESTIONS AND DILEMMAS (OPTIONAL)

If you're inclined to take your work a step further, consider helping someone else resolve a dilemma using their chakra blueprint. Guiding another person through the process will hone your skills. Essentially, this is the same practice, but this time, you'll be the facilitator.

1. Select someone you're familiar with but not deeply connected to; avoid close family members, partners, or best friends. It's crucial to be somewhat unfamiliar with the person so that your analysis does not seem solely based on prior knowledge. The goal is to interpret a person's chakra structure, not to lean on existing insights. While you could select a stranger and operate with minimal data, incorporating known information enhances the dialogue. This balanced familiarity will help you create a detailed and enriched analysis backed by real-life examples.

2. Work with the individual to identify their chakra blueprint. Ask them to complete the questionnaire and discuss their answers, helping you identify their three dominant chakras. Work together to establish their chakra structure. You're not expected to assert yourself with unwavering confidence right away, so don't stress over it; simply ask the other person to listen with empathy, fostering a safe space for both of you.

3. Begin to work through the six steps detailed in the previous practice. This structured approach means there's no need to second-guess your guidance.

   Invite the individual to articulate a question they wish to resolve, a decision they're pondering, or an inner conflict they're navigating.

4. After narrowing down their specific query or dilemma, encourage them to share their internal dialogue, giving voice to their inner conflict and uncertainty.

   As the person shares, write down their statements, highlighting areas where you discern a link to a specific chakra. Sketch three columns and categorize their statements under the corresponding chakra type.

   While the process is collaborative, aim to be the primary guide, especially when linking voices to chakras.

5. When the individual has finished sharing, it is time to aid them in seeking a solution. After listening, categorizing, and interpreting, you might already have intuitive suggestions. Although it's vital to lead assertively, foster a collaborative conversation, ensuring you're attuned to their insights and emotions as well.

6. Transition to the verification phase. Guide the individual to affirm the solution's authenticity by asking themselves questions such as: Does the solution ensure a harmonious flow in line with their soul design? Are all three chakra types correctly positioned and fulfilling their roles? Is there a discernible flow from essence to tangible realization? Does this solution align with their true self, bringing feelings of contentment and joy?

7. Finally, in the visualization phase, direct the individual to envision a detailed scenario in which they have applied their chosen solution. Ask them to share their observations. Does

the scenario resonate harmoniously? How does their body react to it? What's the energy like? Do they feel at peace, complete, and content? Would this solution inspire a change in their actions?

Document the individual's insights, capturing key details.

ELEVEN

CREATING YOUR PERSONALIZED COACHING PROGRAM

As you approach the end of this journey, begin contemplating the path forward. This chapter isn't a recap; rather, it sets the stage for next steps. My personal structure (6–5–3) influences this perspective: life isn't about endings, but perpetual forward motion.

In part III, you explored the chakra blueprint's broader applications beyond basic personality analysis. While you've addressed many of its functions, two pivotal topics remain: first, the approach for unifying and balancing your structure, and second, the approach to achieving this balance through a tailored coaching program.

For you to truly understand these two applications, I must first clarify some key differences. Primarily, there's a notable difference between unifying and balancing—they represent two distinct actions. When I talk about unifying, I'm referring to the optimal utilization of the three inherent energies or powers each of us possesses. These energies are vital for your utmost fulfillment and self-realization. To unify means to effectively harness each of the three chakras individually and synergistically. When each chakra operates in its ideal capacity, it naturally culminates in a unified system. The core requirement is simple: each chakra should function to its highest potential. By doing so, it contributes to the entirety of the structure.

A pivotal aspect of integrating your chakra structure and a coaching program is the recognition of your strengths. A technique I can't emphasize enough in this unification process is recognizing, being deeply conscious of, and cherishing your inherent strengths. Clearly defining and consciously vocalizing your strengths is essential. When you actively acknowledge your strengths, you are empowered to harness them more effectively. Simply knowing isn't enough—you must consciously appreciate and utilize the gifts you possess.

At times, you might become overly engrossed in your blueprint's perceived weaknesses or its "lessons." This can lead to an relentless pattern of dwelling on your challenges, constantly seeking understanding and ways to conquer them rather than embracing your strengths. Many of us inherently possess a mindset rooted in problem-consciousness, which may drive you to focus on what's lacking, what's missing, or what requires correction. This perspective frequently leads to the question "What's the lesson in this?" while continually striving to navigate and learn from experiences.

While recognizing your lessons is vital, it shouldn't overshadow the profound understanding of your innate strengths. It's essential to appreciate the qualities illuminated in a chakra blueprint and harness them for personal evolution and collective benefit. If I was aligned with the root chakra, for example, I shouldn't hastily label myself as slow, boring, and humorless. Instead, I should recognize my dedication, tenacity, loyalty, community spirit, passion for harmony, and deep connection to the tangible world. Hence, it's essential to comprehensively list all of your strengths. This will be explored in the upcoming practice.

Using my own structure (6–5–3) as an example, I was able to identify thirty strengths in a short amount of time. Such a list might seem like an overflow of self-appreciation, but there's no harm in recognizing your worth. From the sixth chakra, I draw upon intelligence, depth, precision, observant capacity, silence, nonattachment, discrimination, mental clarity, alertness, and curiosity. The throat chakra grants me the ability to articulate complex ideas, express myself, radiate charisma, influence others, envision futures, recognize potential, bridge diverse worlds, manifest intentions, and demonstrate leadership. Meanwhile, the third chakra fuels my ambition, focus, determination, dignity, self-discipline, resilience, obstacle navigation, strategic thinking, pursuit of excellence, courage, and energy. Imagine realizing all of your strengths—how empowering would that feel?

Empowerment starts from within. Only you can bestow it upon yourself. Relying on others will be fruitless. Your identity is intricately woven by three dominant chakras and their strengths. I've often heard motivational speakers say things like "You're incredible just as you are" or "Embrace your beauty." However, such statements are vague. It's crucial to recognize the unique ways in which you are exceptional and valuable. Each of us embodies three distinct energies that have an abundance of strengths and intrinsic beauty. You have an innate wealth to offer the world, and it is rooted in who you are, not in who you "might be" or "should" become. This is the heart of this work.

Apart from the quest for unity, there's a principle I call balance. Balance isn't merely about correction. While the word *balance* suggests fixing something amiss, equating it strictly with correction jeopardizes self-acceptance. True self-acceptance is a central benefit of this approach.

Thus, this journey intertwines acceptance and balance. These elements are complementary, not conflicting. Indeed, balance arises from a foundation of self-acceptance and self-love. So, if I observe that my chakra makeup is composed of fire, water, air, earth, or even a mix of these energies that might intensify one another, this doesn't indicate a flaw or problem within me. Instead, it signifies that, like all structures, mine too requires balance and moderation for peak performance.

This is the rationale behind step 2 of the upcoming Designing Coaching Programs practice, in which you will be asked to draft two lists: one detailing the strengths of your three dominant chakras, and the other capturing their weaknesses. Recognizing your weaknesses and limitations is essential in the journey to self-awareness.

Here lies an intriguing insight: *Our perceived "weaknesses" aren't necessarily meant to be corrected.* For example, the third eye chakra type might exhibit bouts of arrogance, while the throat chakra type occasionally displays laziness, but these aren't critical issues demanding correction. If anything, I'd suggest embracing these quirks with a touch of humor and self-awareness. It's therapeutic to acknowledge our flaws with a light-hearted remark, such as "Ah, there's my cheeky arrogance acting up" or "Well, that's just me in one of my lazy moments."

If these aren't problems, you might be wondering why I am going to ask you to compile such a list. This list will allow you to identify specific weaknesses that magnify themselves due to the interplay between the types. Take, for example, the sacral chakra and the solar plexus chakra; both have inclinations toward addictions, obsessions, and unhealthy habits. When they are combined, this tendency intensifies. Recognizing mutual intensifications helps us foresee potential risks, such as a tendency toward self-destructive behavior, health implications, or dysfunctional patterns.

For example, if an individual has completely ungrounded chakras (especially two or more), this increases the likelihood of struggling to fully engage in life's daily functions. If you combine the sixth, fifth, and third chakras (as in my personal example of 6–5–3), there's a potential risk of burnout. A blend of the sacral and heart chakras can sometimes lead to depression, particularly when the heart chakra is predominant. Joining the third, fifth, and perhaps second chakras might foster behaviors that stress or jeopardize close relationships. These are simple examples. It's crucial to recognize and confront these scenarios in a coaching program, given the pressing need for balance in such situations.

However, if you don't detect recurring trends in your list of weaknesses, there's no need for adjustments. When such patterns surface, they often indicate a need for purposeful introspection. Using particular techniques, you can illuminate and improve this facet of your life.

•   •   •   •   •   •   •

By applying the principle of the four missing chakras (introduced in part II) and actively integrating it, you can largely prevent overwhelming imbalances even if your system contains disruptive elements. With a bit of equilibrium and sustained mindfulness, you can keep your chakra structure from going awry and inflicting harm on yourself or others. Integrating the concept of the four missing chakras into your coaching approach can lay a foundation for general well-being, which is the essence of what you're aiming for.

Let's consider the four seemingly "absent" chakras, which almost feels like discussing a hidden treasure. While this framework does suggest the absence of four chakras, it doesn't necessarily mean they're critically missing. As emphasized throughout parts II and III of this book, many of us possess chakras that are nearly as potent as the supportive ones. Hence, you don't necessarily need to categorize any chakras as "missing," considering their abundant presence within you.

In chapters 2 and 4, I asked you to assign a percentage to each of the seven chakra types. Focus on the chakras that you assessed as comprising between 5 percent and 25 percent in your framework. Chakras that accounted for 30 percent or more don't need to be part of your "missing chakras" regimen. With this in mind, examine your less-represented chakras and contemplate ways to actively engage with them. Consider allocating time for specific activities solely to nurture these chakras. Don't force things to an extreme; it should feel organic to you. The "missing" chakras are there to add vibrancy to your life, to bring relaxation to some areas or strength to others.

Take, for example, a chakra structure of 7–4–2. Those with this configuration often have a notable absence of the solar plexus chakra. In practical terms, this could translate to setting a yearly goal of ten objectives you'd like to achieve. By doing so, you're essentially infusing your life with the energy of the solar plexus chakra because you're purposefully aiming for something. Similarly, you could set monthly aspirations to maintain this energy. This is just one way to approach a "missing" solar plexus chakra.

There are three strategies that will allow you to compensate for natural imbalances. I ask you to keep them in mind, as they will become important tools as you interpret blueprints.

- The first strategy is to embrace supportive company. If you find that certain qualities elude you, partnering with someone who naturally possesses them can be invaluable. For example, if the heart chakra's influence seems distant, spending quality time with someone who is deeply connected to their heart chakra can boost your own link to it.

Likewise, if you lack ambition, associating with motivated individuals can be transformative. This notion suggests that sometimes you need an external spark, especially if your inner "fire" seems dim. In situations like these, collaborations can strike a harmonious balance. You don't need to possess every trait; instead, you can find balance with others in a web of interconnectedness. This approach can be profoundly enriching.

For example, to design the perfect business, envision one that encompasses an ideal chakra arrangement. Begin with a solid foundation of Builders, grounding the structure and ensuring smooth, orderly operations. Integrate Caretakers, who create a harmonious and tranquil work environment, alongside Achievers to propel the company forward, ensuring constant momentum. Incorporate Speakers as the voice of the company; they will articulate its values and chart its educational and future goals. Introduce an Artist who can infuse creativity and a touch of imagination. Add Thinkers to provide depth, research, and innovative solutions. Lastly, incorporate Yogis, the soul of the company. They will encourage meditation, serenity, and transcendence. With this model, you'd have an organization that operates effortlessly. As for who would pioneer such an entity, well, don't glance my way. Being a Thinker, I'm here to provide the ideas.

A word of caution is necessary. When you bring others into your circle, you may—perhaps unintentionally—judge or criticize them based on their chakra type. From your perspective, which is shaped by your own chakra type, they might seem insufficiently meditative, less insightful, too somber, or not detail-oriented. But for integration to truly work, it's essential to approach different types with deep humility and let their unique qualities enrich your perspective. Without such humility, this approach to balance is doomed to fail.

- Another approach for achieving balance lies in discerning your ideal environment. The setting in which you reside plays a crucial role. For certain chakra types, solitude can be detrimental to their well-being. For others, bustling urban environments can be overwhelming. Hence, it's vital to determine your best fit. Could it be the city? A rural village? Immersion in nature? Or perhaps a community, an organization, a monastery, a large family, or a solitary lifestyle?

Though society often upholds family life as the key to happiness, for some, this can lead to profound inner distress. Not every path suits everyone. Your quest should be to find an environment that promotes balance and fulfillment. You may need a calming space to counteract agitation, while others might seek environments that invigorate, especially if they are faced with lethargy or self-destructive patterns.

- A third way to achieve balance is through personal introspection and self-work. One can't solely depend on their external environment or the company of others. It's up to you to identify what's lacking in your life and then intentionally cultivate those elements, both within yourself and in your external experiences. For example, if you predominantly resonate with the solar plexus chakra, setting aside time each week to spend with friends—with no ambitions, aspirations, or dreams of grandeur, just genuine connection and sharing—can be beneficial. This practice ensures that you aren't always leaning into your innate tendencies.

It's vital to grasp that "missing" chakras aren't personal deficiencies; they represent fundamental needs shared by all humans. Without addressing these needs, you will remain incomplete as an individual.

It's essential to distinguish between restraining your excesses and compensating for your deficiencies. Excesses are attributes you might overemphasize, which can become exaggerated to the point of appearing caricatured or even absurd. On the contrary, deficiencies are areas you might neglect or possess in limited amounts, leaving essential aspects of your well-being unattended. When working as a coach, it's crucial to recognize that everyone has a diverse spectrum of needs. This includes areas outside of immediate awareness or the blueprint itself. Keeping this in mind is critical, especially considering people's innate tendency to prioritize the needs specific to our type.

· · · · · · ·

Now, the pieces are falling into place. This is your starting point to developing a coaching program. Remember that this is simply a suggestion and not a requirement. If coaching doesn't pique your interest, it's perfectly valid to use the insights from this book purely for your own personal growth.

Practice
· · · · · · · ·
DESIGNING COACHING PROGRAMS
Here are seven steps to shape your coaching program.

1. **Extract actionable insights from your visualization journey.** As you've observed, the origin of a coaching program lies in translating insights from your visualization sessions into actionable steps. Remember when you envisioned an ideal life, harmoniously aligned with your inner structure? With that sense of fulfillment in mind, ponder: What are the necessary actions? Which activities truly reflect the lifestyle you've imagined? Articulating these guidelines becomes intuitive when the vision is vivid (and if it's not, revisit the visualization). So, what's the plan? And how do you actualize it? Aim for clarity and precision as you design, and you'll be off to a promising start with your coaching program.

2. **Construct two lists.** One list should highlight the strengths from each of your three chakra types, and the other should outline their respective weaknesses. They form the foundation of your character and propel you forward. It's crucial to reflect on them, truly embrace their significance, and recognize their service to your unique self.

3. **Review your list of strengths.** How can you intentionally harness these strengths? Essentially, this section emphasizes the wise use of your three dominant chakra energies. It's crucial to understand that your program's essence isn't meant to amend

or improve your chakra structure, but rather to leverage what's already present. Recognizing shortcomings merely aims to strike a balance, not to drive self-improvement. The ultimate goal is to devise a coaching program that directs you toward fulfillment, realization, and the harmonious operation of all three of your chakra types in service of the unified system.

4. **Analyze the three numbers.** Which factors will steer your soul design toward fulfillment? How can each type optimally contribute to the greater good?

    Today, many equate optimal functioning with achieving grandeur or making a significant mark in the world. This mindset has become deeply ingrained in our society. However, the essence of your coaching program shouldn't be defined by such standards of self-fulfillment. This is not about seeking fame or widespread success, but rather about harnessing and optimizing the innate strengths you already possess.

    It's essential to recognize that even individuals with the most idealistic ambitions require practical necessities like income and shelter, unless they're fortunate enough to inherit royal privileges. Beyond these necessities, it's commendable to aspire to contribute to the larger community. Thus, your coaching program should guide you to utilize your talents toward both personal and collective fulfillment. In this context, you should ask yourself: *What can I offer? How can I collaborate? What can I do for the betterment of others?* I find it more impactful to frame the question of work as *How can I serve others?* From this perspective, you naturally align your work with the needs of society, grounding your approach in empathy and sensitivity.

5. **Review the three numbers and determine which purpose or role aligns with this soul design.** Considering your strengths, what purpose or role should your soul pursue in life? Because such introspection can be emotionally charged, consider an

alternative approach: view your attributes as if they belong to someone else, as though they are their characteristics and not yours. Ask yourself, *What guidance would I offer someone exhibiting these characteristics?* Often, it's simpler to provide insights for another, making this an enlightening strategy.

6. **Identify potential overextensions that exist within this design.** Which areas require caution, and how can you exercise this caution? In this step, ask yourself: *What are the excesses inherent in this structure? What should I be wary of, and how can I proceed carefully?*

7. **Identify the gaps in this structure.** How might they be addressed?

Notably, step 7 points to the four "missing" chakras. This step asks you to uncover the deficiencies of this structure and consider ways to address them. Remember, it's often just a touch of these elements that's needed for balance, much like the way a dish may require only a pinch of a certain spice. Think of it as a gentle nudge to incorporate certain aspects, remember "missing" elements, and integrate specific activities into your weekly routine.

After completing this exercise, you can hang this list of strengths on your wall, treating it as a cosmic certificate. These attributes are designed to complement each other, which is why they should be compiled into one cohesive list.

* * * * * * *

I recommend, as your next move, piecing together a vision board to enhance the depth and impact of your coaching program. First, immerse yourself in a detailed visualization. Then, based on this visualization, start constructing a vision board.

This isn't an overnight task. Spend weeks, if necessary, seeking out symbols and images that resonate with the emotions and sentiments unearthed during your visualization. Whether you print these out or draw them, steadily populate your board. By the time you're done, you'll have a visual representation of your inner structure. This tangible form of visualization bridges the subconscious and conscious minds, amplifying its potency.

With that, you're fully versed in the principle of the three-type structure.

CONCLUSION

You embarked on a journey of self-awareness, and my hope is that you've come to realize that chakra blueprints can mysteriously capture the architecture of the soul. Your dominant chakra types may strike you as profound and impressive, and so they will remain with you for many years as compasses orienting you to your life's purpose. Gradually, you can develop the habit of consulting this system, just as you may consult a personality test, astrology, numerology, or tarot cards. None of these systems can offer you a complete insight into your being, but each of them manages to elucidate certain aspects of your makeup and destiny, thus enabling you to add some pieces to the jigsaw puzzle of your soul's journey.

I deeply hope that the chakra blueprint system will turn out to be one of those wise masters that will not only briefly inspire you, but also accompany you on your life's path for years to come. Whenever you come across a dilemma and search deep within for an answer, I hope that your three numbers will come to mind, floating directly from your soul's core. These three numbers will always be there to remind you of the inner codes that instantly align you with your higher wisdom.

If you listen closely to the messages contained within these three numbers at significant moments in your life, you will be able to cling to your primary chakra type. This will help you preserve your authenticity regardless of external voices and remain faithful to your sources of happiness and meaning. By not losing sight of your secondary chakra type, you will confidently navigate the waters of life while keeping your eyes fixed on your ideal path of fulfillment. And whenever you feel energetically and emotionally malnourished or disempowered, always remind yourself of the vital nutrients of your supportive chakra type.

Moreover, try to have a vivid sense of the harmonious interrelations between these three numbers as much as possible. This energetic harmony will mirror the inner harmony that you require in the face of each and every challenge you encounter. Consider keeping an image of your chakra blueprint somewhere until you have fully internalized this vision.

Remaining loyal to your chakra structure is how I understand the notions of listening to your heart and doing what you love. When you are attuned to your dominant chakras, the existential doubt that tends to nestle in the human heart can be dispelled. You will stay connected with a palpable sense of your place in this vast universe.